kitchen garden planner

Written by Darrell Trout

Country Home® Books
Des Moines, Iowa

COUNTRY HOME® BOOKS
AN IMPRINT OF MEREDITH® BOOKS

Kitchen Garden Planner

Writer: Darrell Trout
Senior Associate Design Director: Richard Michels
Graphic Designer: Lyne Neymeyer
Contributing Editor: Jo Kellum
Copy Chief: Catherine Hamrick
Copy and Production Editor: Terri Fredrickson
Contributing Copy Editors: Julie Martens, Karen Weir-Jimerson
Contributing Proofreaders: Mary Pas, Kristen Stagg, JoEllyn Witke
Contributing Photographers: Talis Bergmanis, Laurie Black,
   David Cavagnaro, Rosalind Creasy, Alan & Linda Detrick, Michael Jensen,
   Dency Kane, Peter Krumhardt, Julie Maris Semel, Barbara Martin,
   Frederick Ray, Nancy Rotenberg, Virginia Weiler, Saba S. Tian
Contributing Researcher: Dayna Lane
Illustrator/Plans: Melanie Marder Parks
Indexer: John S. Lewis
Electronic Production Coordinator: Paula Forest
Editorial and Design Assistants: Kaye Chabot, Mary Lee Gavin, Karen Schirm
Production Director: Douglas M. Johnston
Production Manager: Pam Kvitne
Assistant Prepress Manager: Marjorie J. Schenkelberg

MEREDITH® BOOKS
Editor in Chief: James D. Blume
Design Director: Matt Strelecki
Managing Editor: Gregory H. Kayko
Executive Garden Editor: Cathy Wilkinson Barash

Director, Sales & Marketing, Retail: Michael A. Peterson
Director, Sales & Marketing, Special Markets: Rita McMullen
Director, Sales & Marketing, Home & Garden Center Channel: Ray Wolf
Director, Operations: George A. Susral

Vice President, General Manager: Jamie L. Martin

COUNTRY HOME® MAGAZINE
Editor in Chief: Carol Sama Sheehan

MEREDITH PUBLISHING GROUP
President, Publishing Group: Christopher M. Little
Vice President, Consumer Marketing & Development: Hal Oringer

MEREDITH CORPORATION
Chairman and Chief Executive Officer: William T. Kerr

Chairman of the Executive Committee: E. T. Meredith III

All of us at Country Home®
Books are dedicated to providing
you with information and ideas
to enhance your home and garden.
We welcome your comments and
suggestions. Write to us at: Country
Home® Books, Garden Editorial
Department, 1716 Locust St., LN-
116, Des Moines, IA 50309-3023.

If you would like to purchase
additional copies of any of our
books, check wherever books
are sold.

Cover Photograph: John Reed
Forsman

Nothing is quite so satisfying as eating the first sun-ripened tomato or picking the first fragrant leaves of basil fresh from your own garden. And that pleasure is enhanced when the garden is not the run-of-the-mill vegetable garden, with row upon row of crops. Instead, with the help of *Kitchen Garden Planner*, you can create a a beautiful garden that supplies you with the plants you like to use most—vegetables, herbs, fruit, and flowers (edible and ornamental types).

As you browse through this book, you'll see that many of the gardens are primarily herb gardens. That's because people are using herbs more and more in the kitchen and also as medicines, in arrangements, even as dye plants. Some, whose lives run at a frantic pace, use them to enhance convenience foods.

So many people crave the taste of home-grown vegetables and herbs and the relaxed pace of gardening. However, they know little about getting started in this delightful "dirty-knee" pastime. *Kitchen Garden Planner* presents useful gardening information in a format that's accessible and beautiful. Seasoned gardeners will glean plenty of new ideas, too.

For inspiration, look to the first half of the book which presents the gardens. You'll view 13 unique kitchen garden plans, see luscious color photos of each, and meet the gardeners who created each of the gardens. Not only can you mimic the elaborate plan of an established garden, you can also lift key planting combinations and design ideas that adapt best to your own situation.

To simplify your selection of plants, we've included an encyclopedia after every plan. A photograph of each plant is featured, with specific cultural information and growing tips.

Kitchen Garden Planner will serve you well in any region. Even if you don't live in the same area as the featured gardens, the plants represent various hardiness ranges, so you can use most in your own design. Choose key plants for your garden that will come back year after year—fruiting trees and shrubs, or perennial herbs and flowers. Annual herbs and vegetables make up the rest of the garden. You'll be inspired by the diversity of varieties. What's more, the mail-order sources on page 186 make all the plants readily available.

The second section of the book—"Creating Your Kitchen Garden"—is hardworking. It gives you all the information you need to get started and keep your garden growing—from enriching your soil to preserving your harvest. As salads are everyone's favorites, we've devoted extra pages to the many varieties of tomatoes, lettuce, and other greens and how to grow them.

Enjoy creating and growing your garden—from working the earth to discovering the taste sensations fresh from your own kitchen garden.

how to make a kitchen garden

table of contents

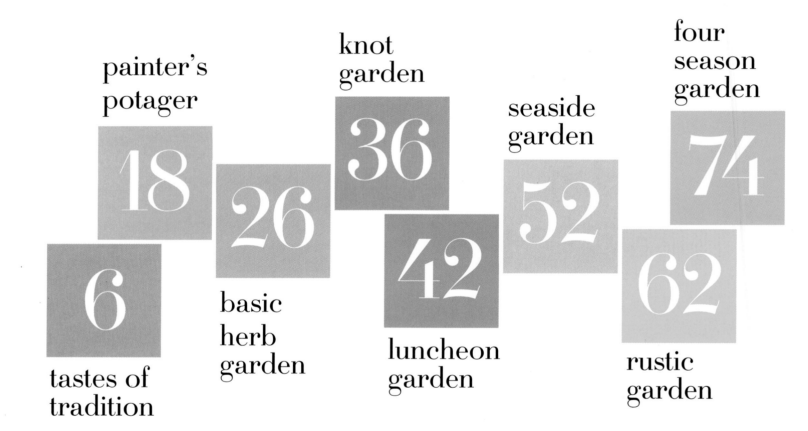

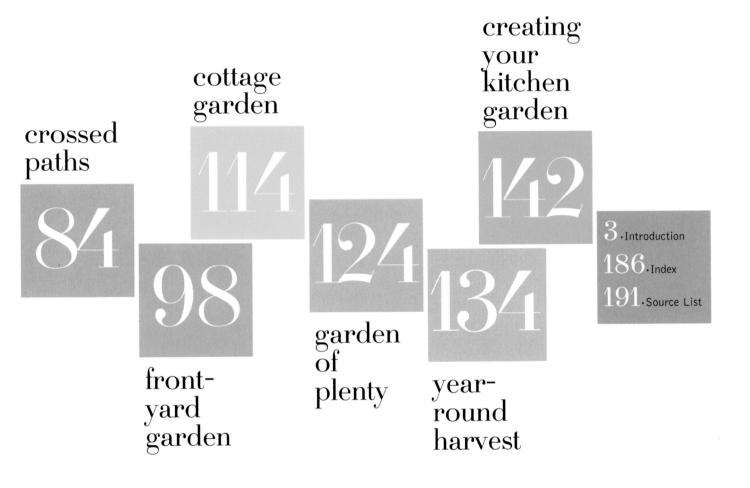

tastes of

tradition

P

rim beds filled with heirloom vegetables and

flowers recall the Colonial roots of gardening

in old Virginia. Owned by the same family since the

18th century, this garden recalls the self-sufficiency of

early settlers while serving

contemporary tastes. Here,

old and new plants flourish

companionably, producing a

harvest of fresh ingredients

for cooking and preserving.

A wooden tuteur will provide support for tomatoes and beans. *Opposite:* Old-fashioned, fragrant sweet peas.

building on family traditions

The journey that John and Marie Butler embarked upon when they built their home on the Butler family property in Chesterfield, Virginia, would take them back to Colonial days. They researched genealogical and horticultural roots to learn more about the heritage of the land owned and planted by John's family since the 1700s. Mindful of their agrarian legacy, the Butlers saw gardening as a way to illustrate the self-sufficiency of generations past.

The Butlers worked the land by cultivating a generous 80×70-foot kitchen garden. John planted an eleagnus hedge on one side; rustic split-rail fencing encloses the remaining three sides and showcases antique climbing roses that Marie imports from all over the world. She also researches and introduces flowers and vegetables from other continents, much like settlers who brought favorite crops with them from the Old World.

It is fitting that John and Marie include plenty of heirloom vegetables in their palette. She harvests flowers of 'Painted Lady' sweet peas—a species which dates from 1737—for both salads and bouquets. Clove pinks sport fringed, two-toned pink blossoms that add sparkle to salads and drinks. Tasty eggplants contribute rich hues to the garden; 'Rosa Bianca' and 'Violetta di Firenze' are Marie's favorite selections. 'Kyoto' mizuna (*Brassica juncea* 'Japonica') quickly became a family favorite for its dainty, billowy appearance in the garden and for the flavor it adds to stir-fry dishes.

The garden itself is shaped with old-fashioned formality. Within the symmetrically shaped beds, flowers and vegetables grow together in a harmonious mix of color and form. Lettuces grow everywhere, prized as much for aesthetic value as for fresh menus. A pair of matching rectangular plots are divided by diagonal rows of lettuce and punctuated by heads of cabbage set like four points of a diamond. Zoysia pathways, as thick as padded carpets, embroider the design.

The splendor of the garden and the plentiful harvests it produces season after season are evidence of John and Marie's deep love of the land. Their children, now living in homes of their own, continue the family legacy as another generation of Butlers tends new gardens grown with a taste of tradition.

Soften the formality of a brick walkway —let plants spill out of the beds. *Opposite:* Overview of the garden.

FRAGRANT OLD ROSES

Old garden roses, once highly prized, went out of favor in the mid 1900s, with the introduction of so many new hybrid roses. Because old roses are so durable, many survived years of neglect in abandoned cottage gardens and are now being propagated and reintroduced.

These vigorous roses frequently boast large numbers of fragrant flowers. They have lush foliage during summer and decorative red hips in fall and winter.

The French rose (*Rosa gallica*), alba rose (*R. × alba*), and damask rose (*R. × damascena*) are among the oldest varieties and figure in the lineage of most of modern roses. Many do not require pesticides to perform well—a necessity when using roses for edible flowers, in crafts, or near vegetables.

The spirit of **early pioneers** lives on, as exemplified by John and Marie Butler. Colonial settlers experimented out of necessity (remember the tomato was still considered poisonous in many parts of the world)—they had no choice but to try unfamiliar species of vegetables and ornamentals. Like their Virginia forebears, the Butlers continually seek out new and unusual plants and vegetables while bringing out the beauty of their garden. Before selecting a plant, they consider its practicality as well as visual appeal. The Butlers insist that even lettuce, down to the most humble varieties, boast pleasing colors and forms.

snap pea

Pisum sativum var.
macrocarpon 'Cascadia'
- Annual
- 2–3' vines
- 58–70 days
- Spring, summer harvest
- Deep green pods
- Sun
- Sources: h, w, ff

Multiple-disease-resistant dwarf variety with high yields. Needs a low fence or trellis.

sweet pea

Lathyrus odoratus hyb.
- Annual
- 1–8'
- Spring, summer
- Wonderful sweet scent
- White to purple

- Sun
- Sources: kk, tt, uu, zz, bbb

Clusters of 1–2" pea–type flowers. Start seeds in early spring, or early fall in mild winter climates; does best in cool weather. Grow on trellis or other support.

batavian lettuce

Lactuca sativa hyb.
- Annual
- 6–12"
- 45–65 days
- Spring, fall harvest
- Rosy leaves
- Sun
- Sources: uu, aaa

Batavian lettuce combines romaine crispness with butterhead shape; has attractive, tasty, colorful leaves; does well in hot weather.

japanese mustard

Brassica juncea var.
rugosa 'Red Giant'
- Annual
- 4–18", taller in flower
- 40–65 days
- Spring, fall harvest

- Yellow
- Sun
- Sources: h, w, ff, ii, kk

Deep purplish red savoyed leaves with mustardy flavor. Pick young leaves for salads—they're milder. Flowers are edible; use in salads, sprinkled on soups.

basil

Ocimum basilicum
'Green Ruffles'
- Annual, herb
- 24"
- Summer, fall
- Aromatic foliage
- White
- Sun
- Sources: e, h, oo, zz, fff

Popular herb used fresh in pesto and wonderful with tomatoes; flowers are edible, too. Deeply cut foliage. Start seeds indoors 4–6 weeks before last frost date.

1. Sweet Pea
2. Snap Pea
3. Batavian Lettuce
4. Japanese Mustard
5. Basil
6. Shrub Rose
7. Hyacinth Bean
8. Foxglove
9. Evening Primrose
10. Moonflower
11. Cottage Pinks
12. Dame's Rocket
13. Climbing Rose
14. Chili Pepper
15. Egyptian Onion
16. Star-of-Persia
17. Oregano
18. Russian Olive
19. Viola
20. Romano Bean
21. Leek
22. Snow Pea
23. Chili Pepper
24. Eggplant
25. Raspberry
26. Savoy Cabbage
27. Cherry Tomato
28. Bush Bean
29. Cucumber
30. Chili Pepper
31. Looseleaf Lettuce
32. Radicchio
33. Shelling Pea

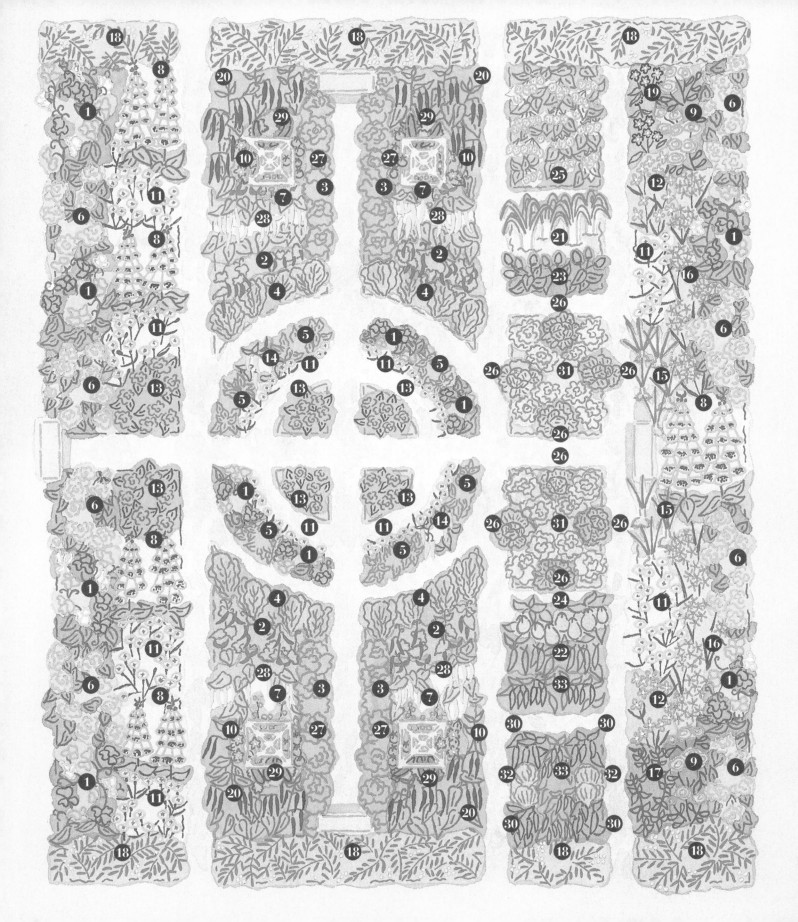

shrub rose

Rosa Mary Rose ™
- Shrub
- 4–5'
- Late spring, fall
- Soft fragrance
- Pink
- Zones 5–9
- Sun
- Source: jjj

David Austin rose with old-fashioned look. Deadhead after first flush of blooms for good fall bloom. Rose petals are edible if not sprayed.

foxglove

Digitalis purpurea
- Biennial
- 3–5'
- Spring of 2nd year
- White to purple
- Zones 4–9
- Part shade
- Sources:kk, tt, uu, bbb

Elegant flowering spikes of bell-shaped flowers; perfect in formal or cottage gardens. Likes moist soil. Let some go to seed to encourage reseeding.

hyacinth bean

Lablab purpureus
(*Dolichos lablab*)
- Annual
- Vine to 30'
- Summer
- Fragrant
- White, purple
- Sun
- Sources: u, uu, ee, kk, tt, bbb

Fast-growing, flowering vine. Decorative purple seedpods (not true beans). Plant seed directly where it is to grow next to a sturdy support.

evening primrose

Oenothera speciosa
(*O. berlandieri*)
- Perennial
- 10–12"
- Spring, summer
- Pink
- Zones 5–10
- Sun
- Sources: l, ee, ii

Lots of delicate blooms; handsome gray foliage. Can be invasive. Drought tolerant.

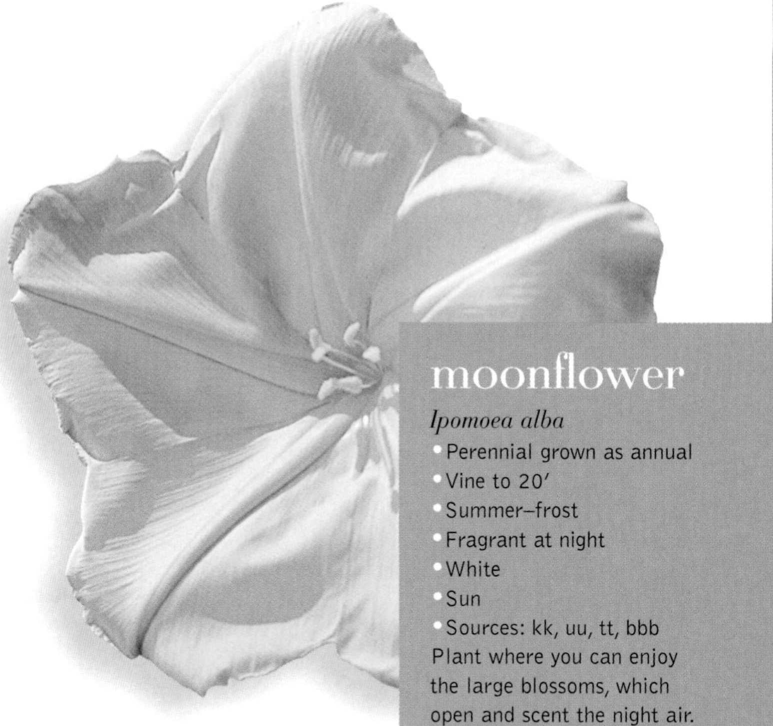

moonflower

Ipomoea alba
- Perennial grown as annual
- Vine to 20'
- Summer–frost
- Fragrant at night
- White
- Sun
- Sources: kk, uu, tt, bbb

Plant where you can enjoy the large blossoms, which open and scent the night air. Soak seed overnight before planting. Needs long, warm summers to bloom.

dame's rocket

Hesperis matronalis
- Biennial or perennial
- 24–40"
- Late spring, summer
- Fragrant
- White to purple
- Zones 3–9
- Sun, part shade
- Sources: ff, kk, oo, tt, bbb

Deliciously scented, particularly at night. Single-flowered form is easy to grow in moist soils. Protect from strong sun.

cottage pinks

Dianthus plumarius hyb.
- Perennial
- 6–18"
- Summer–fall
- Spicily fragrant
- White to rose-pink
- Zones 4–10
- Sun
- Sources: f, u, ii, zz, iii

Long-cultivated favorite. Small single to fully double, often fringed, flowers. Grow in rich, well-drained soil; add lime if your soil is acidic.

climbing rose

Rosa 'Zéphirine Drouhin'
- Shrub, deciduous
- 12–20'
- Spring, fall
- Highly fragrant
- Deep cherry pink
- Zones 6–9
- Sun
- Source: a

Vigorous antique rose; large, semidouble flowers. Thornless; great for a porch column or near a walkway.

chili pepper

Capsicum baccatum var. *pendulum* 'Aji Amarillo'
- Perennial grown as annual
- 2–3'
- Summer harvest
- Orange fruit
- Sun
- Source: hhh

2–3" slender, yellow to orange peppers. Start indoors; transplant outdoors when nights are reliably above 50°F.

egyptian onion

Allium cepa
Proliferum Group
- Perennial
- 20–36"
- Spring, fall
- 120 days (spring-planted), 250 days (fall)
- Zones 5–8
- Sun
- Sources: ff, pp, rr

Interesting looking. Forms bulblets at the top of each stalk, which can be pickled. Use like scallions.

star-of-persia

Allium christophii
- Bulb, perennial
- 24"
- Violet
- Spring
- Zones 4–8
- Sun
- Source: aa

Flowering onion with 8–12-inch spheres of numerous star-shaped flowers. Plant bulbs in the fall. Easy to grow. Needs rich, well-drained soil. Good for cut flowers.

oregano

Origanum vulgare var. *aureum* 'Jim Best'
- Perennial
- 18–30"
- Spring to midsummer
- Golden variegated foliage
- Zones 3–10 (not Deep South)
- Sun
- Sources: oo, fff

Decorative variegated leaves. Edible flowers detract from foliage look.

russian olive

Elaeagnus angustifolia
- Deciduous tree
- 15–30'
- Early-summer flowers
- Very fragrant
- Greenish yellow, small
- Zones 2–6
- Full sun, partial shade
- Sources: b, u

Small tree; can be pruned to use as a hedge. Slender, silver-gray leaves. Tough, hardy, drought-tolerant; doesn't like mild winters or very humid summers. Good bird habitat.

viola

Viola spp.
- Perennial grown as annual
- 6–8"
- Spring (winter in mild-winter climates)
- Purple, yellow, white
- Zones 3–10
- Shade, part shade
- Source: bbb

Small pansy-like flowers, 1–1½ inches across. Prefers moist, well-drained soil. Flowers are edible; wonderful in fruit salads and for decorations on desserts.

romano bean

Phaseolus vulgaris hyb.
- Annual
- 1–6'
- Bush 50–60 days, pole 60–80 days
- Summer–frost harvest
- Green or yellow pods
- Sun
- Sources: e, x, rr

Broad, flat-podded snap beans with meaty texture. Provide support for pole varieties to grow on.

leek

Allium porrum 'Blue Solaise'
- Biennial grown as annual
- 2'
- 100–105 days
- White flowers, blue leaves
- Sun
- Sources: g, rr

French heirloom. Blue leaves turn violet in cool weather. Good for short-season areas; winter harvest. Mulch after frost.

snow pea

Pisum sativum var.
macrocarpon hyb.
- Annual, vine
- 2–5'
- 60–75 days
- Spring, fall
- Sun
- Sources: e, w, ff, ii, aaa

Flat, edible pods; harvest while soft and pliable. Best eaten soon after harvesting. Wonderful in salads and stir-fries. 'Oregon Giant' produces a large, sweet pod.

eggplant

Solanum melongena
'Rosa Bianca'
- Perennial grown as an annual
- 4–6" long fruit
- 75 days
- Summer
- Rosy lavender and white fruits
- Sun
- Sources: ii, uu

Italian heirloom with large, oval fruit. Eggplants are attractive plants that love warm weather.

chili pepper

Capsicum annuum
'Bolivian Rainbow'
- Perennial grown as annual
- 2–3'
- 75 days
- Summer
- Purple, yellow, red
- Sun
- Source: ss

Beautiful landscape plant with purple leaves and brilliant colored, 1" fruit. Productive early and throughout the season.

raspberry

Rubus idaeus 'Fall Gold'
- Shrub, cane fruit
- 5–7'
- Summer, fall
- Soft, gold berries
- Zones 4–9
- Sun
- Source: p

Prolific, self-pollinating producer of unusual, soft, gold berries. Less seedy than red raspberries. First crop in July, then again in September. Remove old canes.

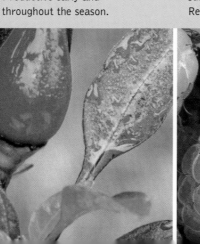

savoy cabbage

Brassica oleracea
Capitata group
'Chieftain Savoy'
- Annual
- 7–10" diameter
- 80–105 days
- Blue-green leaves
- Sun
- Sources: zz, aaa, ddd

Flattened, round, 6–8 lb. heads with finely curled leaves. Excellent flavor. Withstands frost and heat well. Needs rich, well-drained soil.

bush bean

Phaseolus vulgaris 'Goldkist'
- Annual
- To 2'
- 58 days
- Summer harvest
- Bright yellow pods
- Sun
- Sources: q, w

Highly recommended variety for both North and South. Tender, 5–6" long, slender pods on large, upright plant; bean mosaic virus and rust-resistant.

cherry tomato

Lycopersicon esculentum var. *cerasiforme* 'Sun Cherry'
- Annual
- Tall, indeterminate vines
- 58 days
- Summer fruit
- Sun
- Source: w

One of the sweetest cherry tomatoes. The 1½" fruits are held grape-like, up to 20 in a cluster. Will continue to fruit until frost. Pick some green and ripen indoors.

cucumber

Cucumis sativus
'Edmundson'
- Annual
- 4–5' vine
- 70 days
- Summer fruit
- Sun
- Source: xx

Heirloom from Kansas with whitish green fruit; good flavor. Vines are prolific and disease-resistant. Needs lots of water. Heavy feeder; provide ample organic fertilizer.

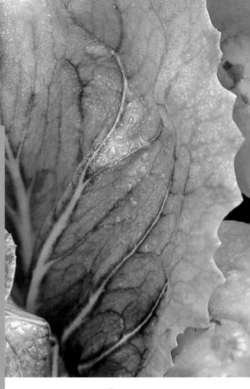

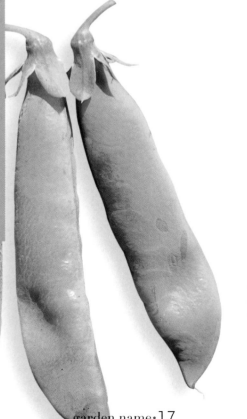

chili pepper

Capsicum annuum
'Rio Grande'
- Perennial grown as annual
- 18–24″
- 85 days
- Summer
- Red fruit
- Sun
- Sources: qq, ss

This medium-hot pepper is a little larger and slightly milder tasting than Jalapeño. Good all-around chili pepper.

radicchio

Cichorium intybus hyb.
- Annual
- 3–6″
- 85–100 days
- Late fall
- Green leaves flushed burgundy
- Sun
- Sources: h, w, kk, oo, uu

Red Italian chicory. Sow in late spring (or fall in zones 8+). If plants do not head up, cut back around Labor Day; they'll resprout and head up for harvest in 4 to 6 weeks.

looseleaf lettuce

Lactuca sativa
- Annual
- 6–12″
- 45–60 days
- Spring to fall harvest
- Green or red leaves
- Sun
- Sources: h, w, ff, uu, aaa

More heat-tolerant than regular head lettuce. Begin planting in the spring, sow weekly, and water generously.

shelling pea

Pisum sativum
'Tall Telephone'
- Annual, vine
- 4–6′
- 68–79 days
- Spring, fall
- Sun
- Sources: kk, rr, zz, ddd,

Very prolific plants produce long pods with 8 or 9 peas. Good for freezing. Peas prefer cool weather; can be planted as soon as the temperatures warm to 50°F.

painter's potager

t he herbs and vegetables, set in a series of defined spaces of this Long Island potager, face tough criteria: They must be sturdy enough to withstand coastal winds yet pretty enough to please a painter's eye. Within each space, exquisite garden scenes are complemented by neutral greens, simple lawns, and an occasional expanse of sky. Like a mat around a painting, the areas of calm colors and soothing textures serve to showcase ornately detailed garden compositions.

robert Dash set out to be a gardener at the tender age of four. He yearned for secret pathways and often dug wild seedlings from the woods to plant in little plots. He grew up mastering the secrets of growing things, taught himself painting along the way, and has spent the last 30-odd years combining his talents to cultivate a windswept 2-acre parcel of land that sits just a mile from the Atlantic Ocean.

The artist in Robert instinctively understood the need for a balanced approach to designing his garden. Movement through the acreage is directed through a series of defined spaces he refers to as "garden compartments."

Tucked away in its own little compartment, a salad garden yields beauty while producing for the table. Geometric lines dominate the design, as crossed paths divide a circular bed like four wedges of pie. Herbs and vegetables grow neatly together, like tiles of a living mosaic. Purple cabbage, onion, spinach, bush basil, eggplant, horseradish, banana peppers, cardoon, and tarragon are but several of Robert's favorites.

Elsewhere in the potager, vignettes are as important as are the vegetables. Row crops don't stand a chance in Robert's garden; only carefully woven tapestries of color and texture will do. He sows tiny red-leafed lettuce among tulip bulbs to welcome spring. Red and white chard, kale, and celeriac are grown as much for their color and leaf shapes as for flavor. Ordinary beans didn't do the job aesthetically, so Robert replaced them with scarlet runner beans, which flaunt orange-red flowers. Being edible never excuses a plant from looking its best.

From inside the house, the potager can be viewed from both the bedroom and bath. Blue trellises and tall plants, such as cardoon and hollyhock, provide privacy from the outside. The opposite side of the potager borders the dog kennel. Few dogs have such a magnificent view.

Robert christened his garden Madoo, Scottish for "my dove." The gentle name belies the windborne salt spray and rough winter storms that attack the site. But the garden grows on. Roses grow here, too—rugged rugosas such as 'Frau Dagmar Hartopp', and 'Roseraie de l'Hay', bloom fearlessly. Such plants earn their place in the garden with a kind of stubborn grace that Robert cherishes.

ARTISTIC COLOR PALETTE

Robert splashes small amounts of strong color throughout his garden. The double U-shaped support at the center of the garden is vibrant blue. A Chinese red lacquer gate finial is eye-catching. Lime green covers a shed door that's visible from inside the beds. Even the roofline of the house is given special treatment—the trim and chimney are painted cobalt blue.

You, too, can add character with color to your garden. Experiment freely—you can always paint over a mistake. Try painting fence posts a vibrant color. Accent finials or decorative elements of a fence with a coat of bright paint. Some gardeners have even spray-painted large grasses, like Eulalia grass (*Miscanthus* spp), when they are dormant in winter. Dried allium heads also make a colorful exclamation in the fall and winter garden when sprayed lilac or pink.

artistic **accents** *attract attention*

Purple cabbage works well in a formal potager with its geometric form. *Opposite:* Overview of the garden.

Medieval and classic artistic and *literary works* feed

Robert Dash's imagination, including medieval and Renaissance paintings, classical writings, and Biblical stories. For example, reading about the fifth-century B.C. Greek adventurer, Xenophon, who described seeing four rectangular shrubbery beds in the gardens of Cyrus the Great, inspired Robert to create a similar garden. A medieval woodcut provided the idea for a turf seat made of tamped meadow sod—resembling one in artwork of the Virgin Mary awaiting the Annunciation. 'Lady Banks' and 'Kiftsgate' roses frame another bench that is backed by a mirror on the shed wall.

1. Italian Broadleaf Parsley

2. Onion

3. Romaine Lettuce

4. Eggplant

5. Mesclun Mix

6. Horseradish

7. Spinach

8. French Tarragon

9. Purple Cabbage

10. Leek

11. Oakleaf Lettuce

12. Dwarf Boxwood

13. Nasturtium

14. Cardoon

15. Cherry Tomato

16. Basil

17. Purple Sage

18. Banana Pepper

onion

Allium cepa
- Biennial, bulb
- 4"–4'
- Harvest summer to fall
- Blooms 2nd spring
- White, pink, purple
- Sun
- Sources: k, w, y, aaa

Prefers cool weather and rich soil. Harvest when tops die down.

italian broadleaf parsley

Petroselinum crispum var. *neapolitanum*
- Biennial
- 12"
- 75 days

- White flowers 2nd year
- Leaves spring through fall
- Zones 5–9
- Sun, partial shade
- Sources: w, q, ff, ii

Grown for its nutritious, flat leaves. Hardy; mulch to overwinter it, or take indoors in a pot. Use the leaves sprinkled over soups, or in casseroles and Italian dishes.

romaine lettuce

Lactuca sativa 'Cimmaron' & 'Medallion'
- Annual
- 10–12"
- 58–68 days
- Spring to fall harvest
- Sun to partial shade
- Sources: 'Cimmaron': kk, ff; 'Medallion': w

'Cimmaron' is a deep red, heirloom romaine with good flavor. It rarely bolts. 'Medallion' is a new romaine with dark green leaves and great taste. Slow to bolt.

eggplant

Solanum melongena 'Purple Blush'
- Perennial grown as annual
- 4–6" long fruits
- 62 days (from transplant)
- Lavender flowers

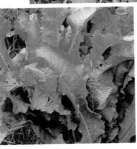

- Summer
- Sun
- Source: e

Lovely oval fruit with a sweet flavor. Start seeds inside; transplant after weather has warmed up well. In mild winter areas with no frost, eggplant may live for years, but most gardeners replant annually for best yields.

mesclun mix

- Annual greens
- To 6"
- Spring harvest
- Sun
- Sources: h, o,m, uu

A mix of salad "greens"—including the richly colored, ruby red radicchio—that are grown to be picked as baby greens or in a cut-and-come-again method.

horseradish

Armoracia rusticana
- Perennial
- 15" first year, 2–3' second year
- Late fall–winter harvest
- Small white flowers
- Zones 4–8
- Sun
- Sources: ii, oo

Grown for its powerfully pungent root. Likes a moist, rich soil, deeply cultivated with all stones removed. Can be invasive, so plant where it will be contained.

spinach

Spinacia oleracea 'Hector'
- Annual
- 6–12"
- 37 days

- Dark green leaves
- Sun
- Source: w

A new hybrid with large, smooth, tender, mild-tasting leaves. It is slow to bolt; resistant to downy mildew.

purple cabbage

Brassica oleracea
Capitata group
- Biennial grown as annual
- 2–7 pounds
- 70–90 days
- Spring, fall harvest
- Purple-red leaves
- Sun or light shade
- Sources: h, q, ii, vv, zz

Beautiful in the garden and on your plate.

french tarragon

Artemisia dracunculus
- Perennial, herb
- 2–3′
- Aromatic foliage
- Dark blue-green leaves

- Full sun to partial shade
- Zones 4–10
- Sources: h, n, oo, fff,

Considered as the true tarragon, it has an anise-like flavor. Needs well-drained soil; divide often. Not good for hot, humid areas. Preserve by freezing, drying, or in white vinegar.

oakleaf lettuce

Lactuca sativa
'Cocarde'
- Annual
- 12″ across
- 49 days
- Spring to fall harvest

- Sun to partial shade
- Source: w

Giant red oakleaf lettuce. Great for baby or cut-and-come-again lettuce. Broadcast the seeds. Pick individual baby leaves or harvest with scissors when about 3–4″ tall.

dwarf boxwood

Buxus microphylla
var. *japonica*
'Kingsville Dwarf'
- Shrub, evergreen
- 2′ high, 30″ wide
- Foliage plant
- Zones 6–9
- Sun or shade
- Sources: g, ww

Compact, rounded shrub. Slow-growing. Tiny dark green leaves.

cardoon

Cynara cardunculus
- Perennial
- 4–6′
- 110–150 days
- Fall harvest
- Silver–gray leaves

- Sun
- Sources: h, ff

Related to artichokes. Grown for its leafstalk— eaten raw or cooked. Popular in Italy and France. Grow in rich soil; keep well-watered and fertilized. Blanch the stalks in the fall.

leek

Allium porrum
'Broad London'
- Biennial grown as annual
- 12–24″
- 80–130 days
- Fall harvest
- Blue leaves
- Sun
- Sources: y, kk, vv

Sweet, mild flavor; also called 'Large American Flag'. Blanch the broad necks by gradually hilling the soil up around them.

nasturtium

Tropaeolum majus
- Annual
- 9–15″ compact, climbing varieties to 8′
- Spring–fall
- Shades of orange, yellow, red
- Sun, partial shade
- Sources: ff, ii, tt, uu, bbb

Easy to grow from seed; likes light, well-drained soil. Sow in early spring, (fall in mild-winter areas). The leaves and flowers are edible— great in salads.

cherry tomato

Lycopersicon esculentum var. *cerasiforme* 'Sweet Million'
- Annual
- 4–6'
- 65 days
- Red fruit in summer
- Sun
- Source: ccc

An improved version of 'Sweet 100'; doesn't crack as easily and is more disease-resistant. Wonderful flavor; high-yielding.

purple sage

Salvia officinalis 'Purpurascens'
- Perennial, shrub
- 18"
- Summer
- Foliage plant—red-purple leaves
- Zones 4–9
- Sun
- Sources: n, oo, fff

Attractive plant. Use leaves for flavoring. Rarely flowers. Requires very well-drained soil or it will rot.

basil

Ocimum basilicum 'Genovese'
- Annual, herb
- 24"
- Summer, early fall
- Aromatic green foliage
- White
- Sun
- Sources: e, h, ff, oo

One of the best basils for pesto; large, flavorful leaves. Likes fertile soil and a warm climate; can grow in pots on a windowsill. Edible flowers.

banana pepper

Capsicum annuum 'Early Sweet Banana'
- Perennial grown as annual
- 2'
- Summer
- 60–65 days
- Yellow to red fruits
- Sun
- Source: jj

Slender, 6" long, Hungarian wax-type, sweet peppers on compact, bushy, early plants.

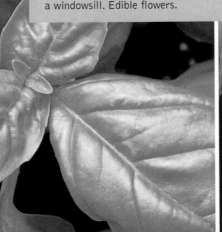

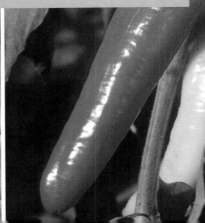

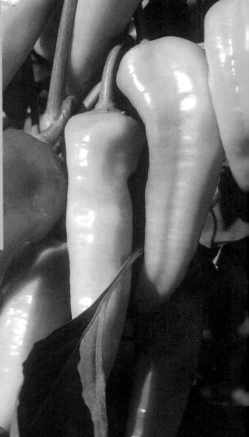

basic

herbs

n

ew England gardeners of years gone by grew just about everything they needed in their own backyards. Herbs played an important role in the Colonial household—their versatility gave rise to gardens of practical themes. This Massachusetts countryside garden recalls nineteenth-century traditions, from cultivating herbs for flavoring and healing to crafting keepsakes such as wreaths, bouquets, oils, vinegars, and other special items.

Charleen Perry and her husband Dan lovingly tend their 32×32-foot plot outlined by a weathered rail fence and patterned with herbs and a sprinkling of flowers. Charleen calls it the "Lady's Household Garden," a nod to the 1800s, when the lady of the house planted what she needed nearby.

Another theme—simple remedies—led to the creation of a pretty little wedge of garden devoted to sage, chamomile, bee balm, thyme, comfrey, and calendula. Rugosa roses grow there, too; Charleen gathers hips rich in vitamin C to steep in tea as a cold remedy.

A culinary garden grows conveniently close to the house, just outside a screened porch.

Summer savory, borage, English lavender, lemon verbena, and sage are a few kitchen favorites.

Each spring, Charleen replaces a few tender plants that don't overwinter, watering the newcomers until established. After that, all herbs are on their own—though the beds are meticulously groomed, watering is left to nature. A 4-inch layer of cocoa bean hulls as mulch minimizes weed growth. The fresh mulch smells delightfully of chocolate; as it ages, mulch adds rich organic matter to the soil.

Harvesting is a happy task. Charleen snips and clips every day from June until frost, taking care to collect herbal foliage before plants bloom for the best-tasting flavors. After removing leaves from the bottom 6 inches of each stem, she gathers the cuttings into bundles and secures them with a rubber band. The rafters of the Perrys' kitchen become a storehouse of bundles hanging upside down to dry.

Some plants are deliberately left to go full flower, so picked blossoms can be added to wreaths and dried arrangements. The stiff, golden flower cushions and ferny foliage of tansy, *Tanacetum vulgare*, make this plant choice for long-lasting dried bouquets. Charleen shares her talents by teaching small classes in her home—the art of making vinegars, oils, potpourris, and holiday decorations using herbs and flowers gathered from the garden. The projects inspire the planting of new herb gardens, so Charleen makes sure her lessons include cultural information and harvesting schedules.

creating a care-free herb garden

ENJOYING HERBS

Growing herbs is almost foolproof. Give them a sunny setting in well-drained soil, and they'll reward you for many years. Grow some between the flowers in a perennial border or in containers. Traditionally, herbs are planted together in beds arranged in formal or geometric patterns. Paths allow easy access to the plants and help contain many herbs that have a tendency to "wander." A few, such as mint, can be aggressive.

If you devote a whole garden to herbs, consider texture, size, and color when selecting plants. Choose contrasting leaf shapes and hues. Place fragrant herbs near paths so you can easily enjoy them. Let a few grow or flop into the paths so that when you brush against or walk on them, their fragrance is released.

Cocoa hulls make rich-looking mulch. Used in paths, they are soft underfoot. *Opposite:* Overview of the garden.

Charleen Perry loves the subdued hues of herbs—

she began her love affair with herbs when she made wreaths for a local craft shop. Silk flowers were popular, but she preferred natural materials. The writings of the late herbalist Adelma Simmons inspired her. A visit to Caprilands Herb Farm, Simmons' Connecticut home and garden, was pivotal for Charleen. Deciding to break from artificial flowers, Charleen spent a week's grocery money on plants and planted her first herb garden. Today, she teaches others to use herbs to add spice and flavor to meals, color to crafts projects, and sweet scents to potpourris.

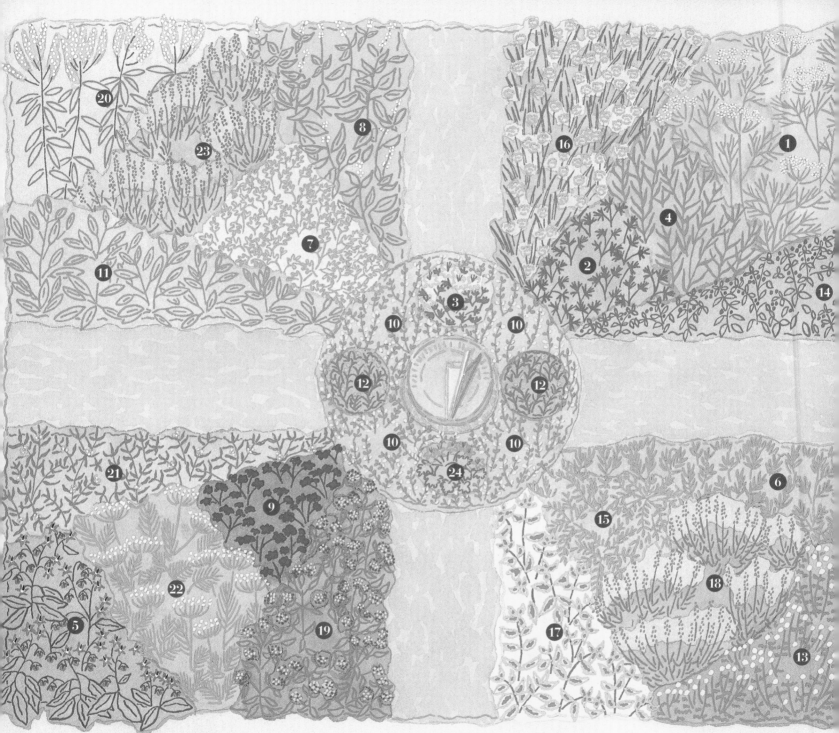

1. Fennel

2. Italian Broadleaf Parsley

3. Lemon-Scented Geranium

4. French Tarragon

5. Borage

6. Artemisia

7. Wormwood

8. Thai Basil

9. Curly Parsley

10. Lime Thyme

11. Sage

12. Pink-Flowered Rosemary

13. Lavender Cotton

14. Sweet Marjoram

15. Artemisia

16. Chives

17. Pineapple Mint

18. English Lavender

19. Oregano

20. Lemon Verbena

21. Summer Savory

22. Dill

23. Spanish Lavender

24. Filbert-Scented Geranium

fennel

Foeniculum vulgare
- Perennial, herb
- 4–5'
- Summer, fall
- Yellow
- Zones 4–10
- Sun
- Sources: w, ii, oo, aaa

Mildly anise-flavored seeds, leaves, flowers, and stems. Attracts butterflies and beneficial insects; favorite host plant for the anise swallowtail butterfly in the West.

italian broadleaf parsley

Petroselinum crispum 'Gigante'
- Biennial
- 24"
- 75 days
- White flowers 2nd year
- Zones 5–9
- Sun, partial shade
- Source: w

Tasty leaves spring to fall.

lemon-scented geranium

Pelargonium crispum 'Prince Rupert'
- Perennial, subshrub
- 3'
- Spring, summer
- Pink
- Aromatic foliage
- Zones 9–10
- Sun
- Sources: n, z, oo

Bushy, upright growth; ruffled leaves; strong lemon scent. Often used in finger bowls; nice in potpourris, sachets.

french tarragon

Artemisia dracunculus
- Perennial, herb
- 2–3'
- Summer
- Greenish white flowers
- Aromatic foliage

- Sun, partial shade
- Zone 4–10
- Sources: h, ii, oo, fff

Anise-flavored culinary herb. Must be cultivated by propagation, not seeds. Rarely flowers. Needs very well-drained, organic soil. Does not do well in humid heat of the South.

borage

Borago officinalis
- Annual, herb
- To 3'
- Spring through fall
- Blue
- Sun
- Sources: ii, oo, tt, fff

Leaves and star-shaped flowers have a mild, cucumber-like flavor. The flowers are beautiful sprinkled on a salad or frozen in ice cubes for summer drinks.

artemisia

Artemisia ludoviciana 'Silver King'
- Perennial
- 2–3' tall, spreading
- Summer
- Yellow
- Aromatic foliage
- Zones 3–8
- Sun
- Sources: oo, fff

Showy ornamental with finely cut, silvery foliage. To use the dried flowers in wreaths, cut while in bud, but before flowers open. Can be invasive.

wormwood

Artemisia absinthium
- Perennial
- 2–4'
- Summer to early fall
- Green flowers, small

- Aromatic, silvery leaves
- Zones 3–9
- Sun
- Sources: n, u, oo

Attractive foliage. Prefers dry, well-drained soil. Not as invasive as some artemisias. Effective as an insect repellent. Caution: toxic—do not eat.

thai basil

Ocimum 'Thai'
- Annual, herb
- 12–18"
- Summer, fall
- Purple
- Aromatic foliage
- Sun
- Sources: w, oo, fff

Handsome purple stems and flowers. Strong anise-clove flavor. Edible flowers and leaves are excellent in Oriental dishes.

lime thyme

Thymus spp.
- Perennial, herb
- 2–12"
- Summer
- Lavender or white
- Zones 5–9
- Sun, partial shade
- Sources: fff, iii

Use creeping lime thyme for a ground cover or in rock gardens. Upright lime thyme is best for culinary uses. Needs a light, well-drained soil; do not overwater.

curly parsley

Petroselinum crispum
- Biennial grown as annual
- 10–18"
- Flowers 2nd year
- White
- Sun, partial shade
- Sources: q, w, ff, ii

Underutilized edible. Tolerant of cold and some frost. Soak seed overnight before planting.

sage

Salvia officinalis 'Berggarten'
- Perennial, herb
- 24"
- Summer
- Nonflowering
- Zones 4–9
- Sun, light shade
- Sources: oo, fff

Broad, low-growing culinary sage with large gray-blue leaves. After drying, sage keeps better in the freezer.

pink-flowered rosemary

Rosmarinus officinalis
- Evergreen shrub
- 2–4'
- Winter, spring in West
- Fragrant
- Pink
- Zones 8–10
- Sun, partial sun
- Source: fff

Great for cooking or drying. Once established, needs little water. Can withstand hot sun, poor soil, ocean spray. Must have good drainage.

lavender cotton

Santolina rosmarinifolia (*S. virens*)
- Evergreen shrub
- 2'
- Summer
- Yellow
- Aromatic foliage
- Zones 6–9

- Sun
- Sources: oo, eee, fff

Shear back to a few inches in early spring. Deadhead the button-like flowers after blooming. Needs good drainage; may not do well in humid heat.

sweet marjoram

Origanum marjorana
- Perennial, herb
- 12"
- Late summer, fall
- White or pink
- Zones 7–9
- Sun
- Sources: h, w, ii, oo, aaa

Mild oregano flavor; edible flowers. Used in French, Italian cuisines.

artemisia

Artemisia ludoviciana 'Powis Castle'
- Perennial
- 2–3', spreading
- Flowers insignificant
- Aromatic, silvery foliage
- Zones 4–8
- Sun
- Sources: f, eee, ggg, jjj

Great foliage plant. Takes the humid heat of the South better than most artemisias. Can be grown in a container.

chives

Allium schoenoprasum
- Perennial, bulb
- 12–18"
- Early summer
- Lavender
- Zones 3–9
- Sun
- Sources: ii, kk, oo, vv, zz, aaa

Pretty grass-like leaves with attractive, edible flowers. Mild onion flavor. Cut back after flowering.

pineapple mint

Mentha suaveolens 'Variegata'
- Perennial, herb
- 16"
- Summer
- White
- Foliage has fruity aroma
- Zones 5–9
- Sun, partial shade
- Sources: oo, fff

Decorative, sweet-smelling mint. Edible flowers are great in syrup or salsa. Sprinkle on vanilla ice cream for a minty taste treat.

oregano

Origanum laevigatum 'Herrenhausen'
- Perennial, herb
- 18–30"
- Spring to early fall
- Pale lilac
- Zones 7–10
- Sun
- Sources: e, n, oo, fff

Attractive, fruit-scented oregano. Leaves are blushed with purple when young and in winter. Edible flowers.

english lavender

Lavandula angustifolia
- Shrub, herb
- 3'
- Summer
- Fragrant flowers and foliage
- Violet-blue
- Sun
- Zones 5–10
- Sources: eee, ggg, jjj

Silvery foliage. Flowers great dried; cut fresh to maintain color. Needs well-drained soil.

lemon verbena

Aloysia triphylla
- Shrub, tender
- 3–6'
- Summer
- Fragrant
- Pale pink
- Zones 8–11
- Sun, part shade
- Sources: z, ff, oo

Wonderful, lemon-scented and flavored leaves; used in teas and potpourri. Well worth growing as an annual in colder climates.

summer savory

Satureja hortensis
- Annual, herb
- 10"
- Summer
- Pink
- Sun
- Sources: ii, oo, fff

Leaves and flowers edible; flavor more delicate than winter savory; best when picked in early summer. Mulch to keep plants clean.

spanish lavender

Lavandula stoechas
- Perennial, herb
- 2–3'
- Summer
- Fragrant
- Dark purple
- Zones 8–10
- Sun
- Sources: oo, fff

Also called French lavender. Check the botanic name to be sure you get what you want.

dill

Anethum graveolens
- Annual, herb
- 36"
- Summer
- Yellow
- Sun
- Sources: e, ii, oo, fff

Ferny leaves and yellow edible flowers are beautiful in the garden and delicious in the kitchen. Enhances many foods; especially tasty with fish. Requires well-drained soil.

filbert-scented geranium

Pelargonium spp.
- Perennial, subshrub
- 1–3'
- Spring, summer
- Rosy pink
- Aromatic foliage
- Zone 9–10
- Sun
- Sources: n, z, oo

Compact form. More tolerant of hot, humid weather than most pelargoniums.

knot

garden

Knot patterns have their roots in the decorative arts, which pre-date the Middle Ages. By the 16th century, geometric knot gardens planted in elaborate designs became popular. Formal patterns were created with foliage plants set closely together. The formal design of this western North Carolina herb bed was adapted from ideas of the past to suit the present. Herbs and handmade floral crafts are for sale; the gardens are free for strolling.

dick and Diane Weaver searched the Blue Ridge Mountains for their century-old farmhouse. With character hammered into every here, they grow a banquet of tastes. Roman chamomile, hyssop, parsley, thyme, rosemary, lavender, and golden sage are just the beginning of the Weavers' plant list. Plentiful harvests provide for personal use and supply their business endeavors.

Dick in the garden—he spends 10 to 12 hours a day working in the garden and greenhouse. He's more than willing to share the history of the herbs at hand. Fresh graces a circular bed at the garden's center. Miniature hedges of lavender cotton, and English and French lavender weave over and under one another. The neatly-trimmed squares and curls intersect, looping around rosemary and sweet bay topiary standards.

viewing texture through design

board, and over an acre and a half to call their own, the Weavers' homestead boasts inherent charm. Diane, an art director by profession, spent the first winter in their new home putting garden schemes down on gridded artist's paper. When spring came, the couple brought her plans to life.

A stroll through the garden reveals the plants' obvious aesthetic value. They named their little world "Gourmet Gardens." Both Dick and Diane love to cook with herbs;

Both Dick and Diane experiment constantly in the kitchen as they prepare to answer frequent questions about the culinary value of herbs.

Visitors come from all over to browse through the greenhouse, stroll the garden paths, and discover herbs and other treasures for sale in the small shop attached to Dick and Diane's home. Guests will usually find

herbs for sale are ready for planting. Each plant is propagated by hand and custom-potted— patrons choose their own pots.

Diane's design shows the beauty of varying colors and textures of foliage and flowers. A formal knot garden

The precision of the bed contrasts beautifully with an Appalachian-made twig bench, gravel paths, and thick, muscular vines coiling their way up trees that date back, perhaps, to the days when the old farmhouse was new.

CREATING A STANDARD
A standard is a specially pruned topiary that can be used in a knot garden, formal garden, or to anchor both sides of a walkway. Grown on a single stem, it's shaped in a rounded, tightly grown mass of foliage. Trees, shrubs, roses, and many perennials can be grown this way.

Start with a plant that is as tall as you want your finished standard. Prune until there is one sturdy stem with a rounded mass on the top. Use a stick or stake to tie the stem into an upright and straight position. Pinch the growth at the top until you've achieved the desired result.

Try bay, rosemary, or boxwood. You also can purchase standard roses, conifers, or other small trees to make standards.

A twig bench is the perfect place to sit and contemplate the knot garden. *Opposite:* Overview of the garden.

Dick and Diane Weaver developed skills with herbs

when they retired several years ago and set sail south on the Intracoastal Waterway. On board, they loved growing and cooking with herbs. When their 40-foot boat was in port, they would move their pots of herbs to the sunny deck. They soon became known as the "herb people"—they even exchanged herbs for fish with a chef in the Bahamas. After two years on the water, they began their search for an herb-friendly climate. They finally settled in the North Carolina mountains and began building their herb garden and business, setting sail for a whole new lifestyle.

english lavender

Lavandula angustifolia 'Munstead'
- Shrub
- 12–18″
- Summer
- Fragrant
- Lavender
- Sun
- Zones 5–10
- Sources: s, eee, ggg, jjj

Compact; plant several for a low-growing hedge. Leaves and flowers edible.

rosemary

Rosmarinus officinalis 'Blue Boy'
- Shrub, evergreen
- 24″
- Winter, spring
- Fragrant
- Light blue

- Zones 8–10
- Sun, partial shade
- Sources: n, oo, fff

Smaller rosemary good for containers. Fertilize with fish emulsion. Use rosemary leaves and flowers for cooking; especially nice with lamb or chicken.

lavender cotton

Santolina chamaecyparissus
- Evergreen shrub
- 2′, spread to 4′
- Summer
- Aromatic foliage
- Yellow
- Zones 6–9
- Sun
- Sources: n, oo, eee, fff

Drought-tolerant. Needs good drainage; prefers lean, sandy soil. Prune off the button-like flowers after they've finished blooming.

sweet bay

Laurus nobilis
- Evergreen shrub or tree
- 12″–40′
- Spring
- Greenish yellow
- Aromatic foliage
- Zones 8–10
- Sun, partial shade
- Sources: n, nh, vv

The source of traditional bay leaves for cooking. Needs moderate water, good drainage. In cold areas, grow in a container and move inside for winter.

rosemary

Rosmarinus officinalis
- Shrub, evergreen
- 3–4′
- Winter, spring
- Fragrant
- Lavender blue
- Zones 7–10
- Sun, partial sun
- Sources: n, s, oo, eee, fff

Tender perennial; grow as an annual in containers. Needs moderate to little water.

rosemary

Rosmarinus officinalis 'Tuscan Blue'
- Shrub, evergreen
- To 6′ tall, 4′ wide
- Winter, spring
- Fragrant
- Blue-violet
- Zones 8–10
- Sun, partial sun
- Sources: n, iii, fff

Dramatic upright plant, with long branches growing up from the base. Rich green needle-like leaves with pinelike fragrance.

1. Rosemary
2. English Lavender
3. Lavender Cotton
4. Sweet Bay
5. Rosemary
6. Rosemary

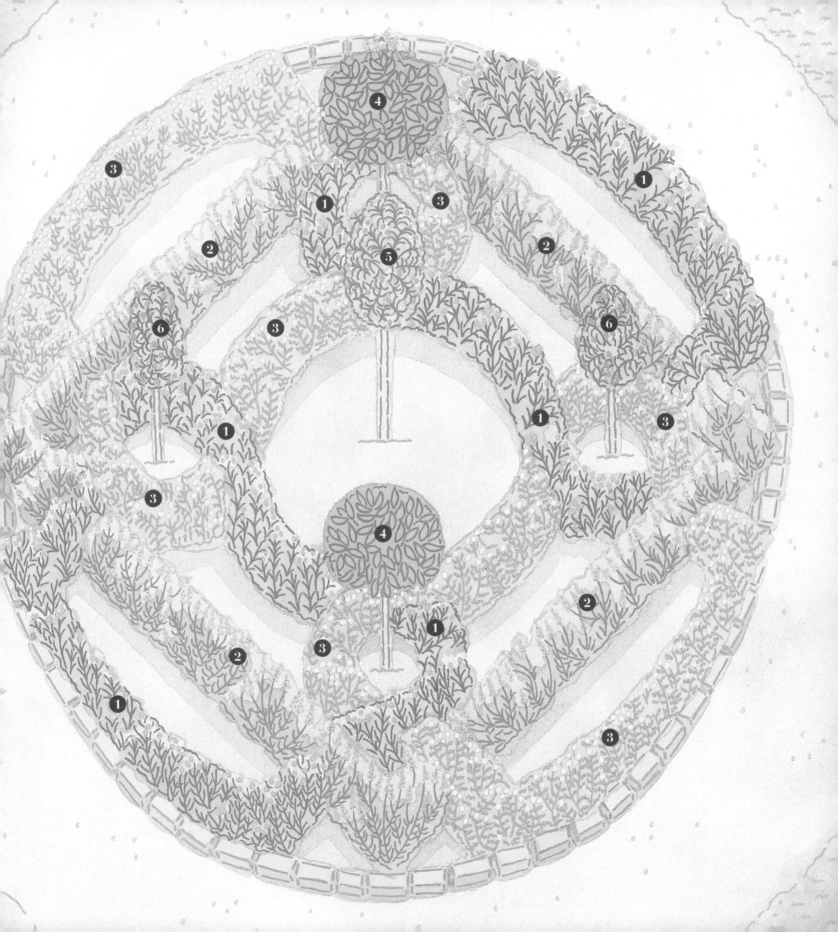

luncheon

garden

P

econic River Herb Farm, like the hand-honed wooden

supports and buildings that grace the property, has been

carved out of the woodland along the banks of the

Peconic River on Long Island. Alive with native flora,

hard-to-find plants, and wildlife,

the bucolic setting draws

many visitors from the city.

Somewhat hidden, the luncheon

garden is a perfect spot for a

simple repast or afternoon tea.

Fresh from the garden: cut flowers, garlic, and herbal vinegars adorn a table. *Opposite:* 'Ruby' Swiss chard.

down a quiet, rutted, dirt road near Calverton, New York, at the eastern end of Long Island, Peconic River Herb Farm stands apart from the business of city life.

children's garden, beginners' herb garden, scented garden, butterfly garden, a "Garden for All Thyme," and garlic. The farm is noted for its annual garlic festival in September. To keep the farm in harmony with nature, all the gardens are cultivated organically.

The luncheon garden is inviting. Guests can savor their elegant surroundings while sipping local wine. The garden changes with the seasons—pole beans may soften the teepee's rigidity in early summer,

the beauty of many edibles in the garden. Red and green orach, dramatic relatives of spinach, date back to ancient Greek and Roman gardens. Cooks like to use young orach leaves in salads. Another decorative edible, 'Bright Lights' Swiss chard, glows at sunset with its rainbow hues.

creating a shaded, casual eating area

Herbs, heirloom flowers and vegetables, everlastings, aquatic plants, wildflowers, garlic, roses, and grasses grow in profusion. From their harvest, owners Cris and Mike Spindler supply their own food and flowers and still have plenty to sell.

On the 13-acre farm, three acres are under cultivation and four are wetlands. The remainder is given over to living space, barn (which serves as shop, drying area, and classroom), and poly greenhouses. Diverse gardens dapple the property, including a

actually a square within a square—a hideaway surrounded by edible plantings—that's a perfect spot for lunch or a cup of herbal tea. A white picket fence anchors the garden, while a teepee of metal reinforcing rods, covered with pole beans, reaches skyward. A green table and ice-cream chairs, arranged on hard-packed soil covered with wood-chip mulch, are

while later in the season, cheery morning glories clamber up the bars.

Edibles are Cris's first choice for the luncheon garden. Annuals vary from year to year so she can try new varieties. These crop rotations also promote healthy growing conditions. Cris relishes

It's easy to catch the scent of roses and dianthus. And, on hot, sunny days, passersby detect Greek oregano, summer savory, and thyme. Cris's favorite herb, lavender, is versatile— beautiful for landscaping and useful in cooking, skin care, and crafting.

GROWING GARLIC
To grow high-quality garlic, Cris Spindler suggests the following:
• Use seed stock from a grower rather than supermarket garlic.
• In autumn, plant the largest cloves, with the tips up, 2 inches deep and 6 inches apart in rich garden soil that receives full sun.
• Weed and water regularly.
• Feed garlic with granular organic fertilizer when planting and again in April and May.
• Harvest in early to mid-July when the tops begin to yellow.
• Leave tops on bulbs. Bundle 12 together and hang for three or four weeks in a dry, airy, cool place.
• Save the biggest bulbs for seed.

Fragrant edible flowers of rose, dianthus, and thyme grow organically. *Opposite:* Overview of the garden.

Cris Spindler's **enthusiasm** for gardening goes back to her childhood. By age 15 she had her own garden where she grew potatoes, spinach, and herbs. She grew to love herbs for their fragrance, ease of cultivation, and what she could make from the plants, including dyes and teas. Their history, folklore, and use in cooking and medicine made them more fascinating than a bed of impatiens. Chis wanted a greenhouse so she could grow more herbs. To pay for it, she started selling plants—Peconic River Herb Farm was born. Today Cris continues her gardening traditions while searching for new and unusual plants, and sharing her enthusiasm with visitors to the farm.

1. Swiss Chard
2. Green Orach
3. Woolly Thyme
4. Looseleaf Lettuce
5. Red-Leaf Amaranth
6. Romaine Lettuce
7. Summer Savory
8. Pole Beans
9. Head Lettuce
10. Greek Oregano
11. Red Creeping Thyme
12. False Sunflower
13. Red Orach
14. Red Perilla
15. Summer Squash
16. Peony
17. Pinks
18. Shrub Rose
19. Nasturtium
20. Hollyhock
21. Signet Marigold
22. Johnny-Jump-Up
23. Rose Campion

green orach

Atriplex hortensis
- Annual
- To 6'
- Harvest spring–summer
- Green foliage
- Sun
- Sources: m, rr

Plant seeds in early spring; start harvesting leaves in 6 weeks. Pinch back regularly and harvest into summer. If not pinched, it will go to seed.

swiss chard

Beta vulgaris 'Ruby'
- Biennial grown as annual
- 18"
- Harvest spring–fall
- Colorful stems, midribs
- Sun
- Sources: q, w

Vividly colorful—red ribs and veins in dark green leaves. Color fades after cutting if in air too long. Cut stems into matchstick sizes and sprinkle over a salad just before serving.

red-leaf amaranth

Amaranthus tricolor
- Annual
- 12–18"
- Summer harvest
- Green and purple leaves
- Sun
- Sources: w, nn

A hot-weather green. Likes rich, well-drained soil. Use young leaves raw in salads, or cook as you would spinach.

looseleaf lettuce

Lactuca sativa 'Red Butterhead'
- Annual
- 6–8"
- 60–75 days
- Harvest spring, fall

- Bronze-tinged leaves
- Sun
- Sources: h, w, kk

Attractive leaves. Butterhead lettuces form a loose head of very tender leaves. Some have been bred for more crispness than other looseleaf lettuces.

summer savory

Satureja hortensis
- Annual, herb
- 10"

- Summer
- Pink
- Sun
- Sources: ii, oo, fff

Called the bean herb. Cook with fresh or dry beans to add richness to the flavor. A warm-season annual, it's easily grown in most parts of the country.

woolly thyme

Thymus pseudolanuginosis
- Perennial
- 2–3", creeping
- Midsummer
- Lavender-pink
- Zones 5–9
- Sun
- Sources: n, oo, fff

Ornamental thyme, not usually for culinary use. Nice ground cover for small spaces—use in rock gardens, between stepping stones.

romaine lettuce

Lactuca sativa
- Annual
- 10–12"
- 66–83 days
- Harvest spring to fall
- Sun to partial shade
- Sources: e, h, w, ii, uu

Also called Cos lettuce. Long, upright, crispy leaves. Prefers fertile, moist soil with added compost. Fertilize with fish emulsion.

pole beans

Phaseolus vulgaris
'Garden of Eden'
- Annual
- 1–6'
- 65 days
- Harvest summer–frost

- Sun
- Source: w

Flat green pods with sweet flavor. Grow pole beans on a trellis or other support. Plant 1" deep, 3" apart. Thin to about 6" apart.

head lettuce

Lactuca sativa
'Summertime'
- Annual
- 10"
- 70–82 days
- Summer harvest
- Sun
- Sources: kk, aaa

Medium-sized; matures in summer's heat without bolting. Good, crispy texture and flavor. Resistant to tip-burn.

greek oregano

Origanum vulgare
ssp. *hirtum*
- Perennial, herb
- 12–28"
- Summer to fall
- Rosy pink
- Aromatic leaves
- Zones 5–10
- Sun, partial shade
- Sources: n, oo, fff

One of the best culinary oreganos; spicy flavor, furry leaves. Plant in well-drained soil. Propagate by divisions or cutting. May not do well in humid heat.

red creeping thyme

Thymus serpyllum
(*T. praecox* ssp.
arcticus) 'Coccineus'
- Perennial
- 1–4"
- Summer
- Fragrant

- Crimson
- Zone 4–9
- Sun
- Sources: n, ii, oo

Forms a dense mat of aromatic foliage and flowers. Use as a groundcover or between stepping stones where you can appreciate the fragrance.

false sunflower

Heliopsis helianthoides
ssp. *scabra*
'Summer Sun'
- Perennial
- 3' tall, 2–3' spread
- Summer–frost
- Golden yellow
- Zones 4–9
- Sun, light shade
- Sources: u, iii

Bright single or semi-double 2–4" blossoms. Excellent cut flowers. Divide every few years.

red orach

Atriplex hortensis 'Rubra'
- Annual
- To 6', seed spikes
- 37 days
- Harvest spring, summer
- Red foliage
- Sun
- Source: m

An heirloom "green" that grows well in hot weather. Can be grown as a cut-and-come-again baby green. Few pests and diseases. Great in a mixed salad.

red perilla

Perilla frutescens
- Annual
- 2–3'
- Summer
- Pink flowers

- Aromatic
- Sun, partial shade
- Sources: h, j

Very popular in Japan. Young purplish-red leaves and shoots are used as a flavoring or garnish. Mild cinnamon-mint scent. An attractive bedding plant. Self-sows.

summer squash

Cucurbita pepo 'Yellow Crookneck'
('Early Summer Yellow')
- Annual
- 24–30"
- 48–58 days
- Summer
- Yellow
- Sun
- Sources: d, m, xx

Bush-type squash. Best picked at
4–6". Edible flowers often stuffed.

peony

Paeonia lactiflora hyb.
- Perennial, long-lived
- Late spring, early summer
- 2–4′
- Fragrant
- White to red
- Zones 3–8
- Sun
- Sources: f, eee

Old garden favorite. Splendid 3- to 4-inch flowers; single to double. Richly perfumed. Requires deep, rich, organic soil and full sun.

shrub rose

Rosa 'Simplicity'
- Shrub
- 5′
- Spring to fall
- Light fragrance
- Pink
- Zones 5–9
- Sun
- Source: v

Lots of continuous blooms. Makes an attractive, quick-growing hedge. Rose petals are edible if not sprayed with pesticide.

pinks

Dianthus hyb.
- Perennial
- 6–18″
- Summer–fall
- Spicily fragrant
- White to red
- Zones 4–10
- Sun, light afternoon shade
- Sources: f, u, ii, zz, iii

Perfect for old-fashioned tussie-mussie bouquets. Edible flowers. Deadhead in summer for fall bloom. Doesn't do well in humid heat of the South.

nasturtium

Tropaeolum majus 'Peach Melba'
- Annual
- 10″, mounding
- Spring to fall
- Creamy yellow, reddish blotches at throat
- Sun, partial shade
- Sources: uu, bbb

Best in cool weather; looks washed-out when hot. Edible leaves and flowers. Shepherd's is creamy yellow; Thompson & Morgan's is dark peach.

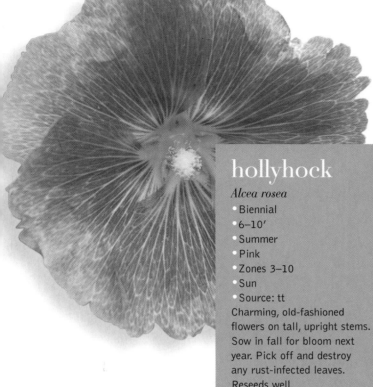

hollyhock

Alcea rosea
- Biennial
- 6–10'
- Summer
- Pink
- Zones 3–10
- Sun
- Source: tt

Charming, old-fashioned flowers on tall, upright stems. Sow in fall for bloom next year. Pick off and destroy any rust-infected leaves. Reseeds well.

johnny-jump-up

Viola tricolor
- Perennial grown as annual
- 6–12"
- Spring, summer
- Purple, yellow, and white
- Sun, shade
- Zones 4–10
- Sources: w, ii

Blooms in winter in mild-winter areas. Self-sows. Small, cheery, edible flowers. Use to liven up a salad or as garnish.

signet marigold

Tagetes tenuifolia 'Lemon Gem' & 'Tangerine Gem'
- Annual
- 8"
- Summer
- Yellow, orange
- Sun
- Sources: h, w, uu

Small, bright-colored single flowers. Needs moist, well-drained soil. The petals are edible in moderate amounts.

rose campion

Lychnis coronaria
- Perennial
- 18–36"
- Summer
- Magenta
- Zones 3–10
- Sources: u, tt

Spreading, silvery, woolly leaves are a foil for bright flowers. Grows best in poor, well-drained soil. Short-lived, but will self-sow.

seaside

garden

In mild, coastal Pacific Northwest weather, clematis and hydrangeas grow happily. *Opposite*: Inula

W

hen it comes to gardening, nature is often the best teacher. A streak of strong will and perseverance doesn't hurt either. This kitchen garden and nursery in coastal Washington State grew from a lifelong passion for studying and experimenting with plants. Valuable trial-and-error lessons made the dream of opening a nursery a reality. Unusual and easy-to-grow plants mix readily with plants that provide food and shelter for birds and butterflies.

in Alaska, Mary Fisher's neighbors begged to buy plants right out of her front yard. When Mary and her husband Tom left Alaska and purchased 23 acres of partly wooded property on Whidbey Island, Washington, she took a bold step. Mary set up shop, calling her enterprise the Cultus Bay Nursery & Gardens.

She reasoned that what she didn't already know, she would learn along the way. Hobby gardening since she was a child, Mary had a broad base of gardening skills.

That was a decade ago. Joining numerous plant societies and seeking out teachers at local colleges gave her access to the expertise of others. Intensive work, from growing everything from species columbines and unusual lavenders to gangly mullein (*Verbascum olympicum*), has given Mary priceless, hands-on experience. She has amassed a unique collection of plants over the years. Antique double ranunculus, double green plantain (*Plantago major*) 'Rosularis', unusual hellebores, and species gladiolus are a but a few of her current favorites.

Herbs remain the utmost of her passions. Today, Mary shares her own knowledge. Visitors to the nursery and garden receive impromptu lessons; others sign up for on-site classes. Mary's classes cover a range of topics, with herbal medicines being one of the most popular subjects.

Like many gardeners who like to cook, Mary chose to site her herb garden near the house. When culinary herbs are within arm's reach (or a few steps) of the kitchen, the cook of the household is more likely to use them. Mary's herbs grow gloriously close at hand in a section of the garden divided into four quadrants by gravel paths. Boxwood borders trim the beds with rows of greenery throughout the year. But far from being formal, the herb plantings themselves are sweet and airy, as though they were the setting of some happily-ever-after fairy tale. Licorice grows beside santolina and lavender; chamomile between golden sage and dwarf hyssop. Russian sage snuggles up next to a clump of tricolor sage. Uncommon nepeta, monarda, and inula mix with everyday favorites such as rosemary, tarragon, and thyme.

Tom built the Fishers' home and now contributes handmade wooden trugs to the nursery's offerings. Daughters Leah and Brita, and son Andrew soak up lessons of the nursery business as a matter of course. Perhaps the value of natural experience and a touch of stubborn faith have taken root, too.

making a dream become reality

SAGE ADVICE

Sage has been linked with longevity and even immortality for centuries. The aphorism "Why should a man die, when he can go to his garden for sage?" dates to the 10th century. The genus name, *Salvia*, is Latin for "salvation."

Even if its powers are overstated, sage is an important culinary and ornamental herb. The pleasantly bitter, lemony, camphorlike flavor is well known. A Thanksgiving turkey wouldn't be the same without sage dressing. Use fresh young leaves of *Salvia officinalis*, culinary sage, in salads or for cooking—try them with pork, poultry, and squash. Fresh leaves are preferred over the commercially available dried product, as they have a more distinct, lemony flavor and lack bitterness.

Mary Fisher's dreams and skills converged to create

Cultus Bay Nursery & Gardens, her home, garden, and business on Whidbey Island, Washington. Her longtime love of gardening and a self-reliant attitude made the 23-acre dream spot possible. She had a vision of what she wanted to do and made it happen. With a strong foundation—she had gardened since childhood, and nurtured plots of eye-catching flowers while in college—Mary set out to learn more, seeking out local experts and joining plant societies. Today, new gardeners benefit from Mary's knowledge and vision. She steers them to foolproof plants, and brings new cultivars and specialty plants to new gardeners.

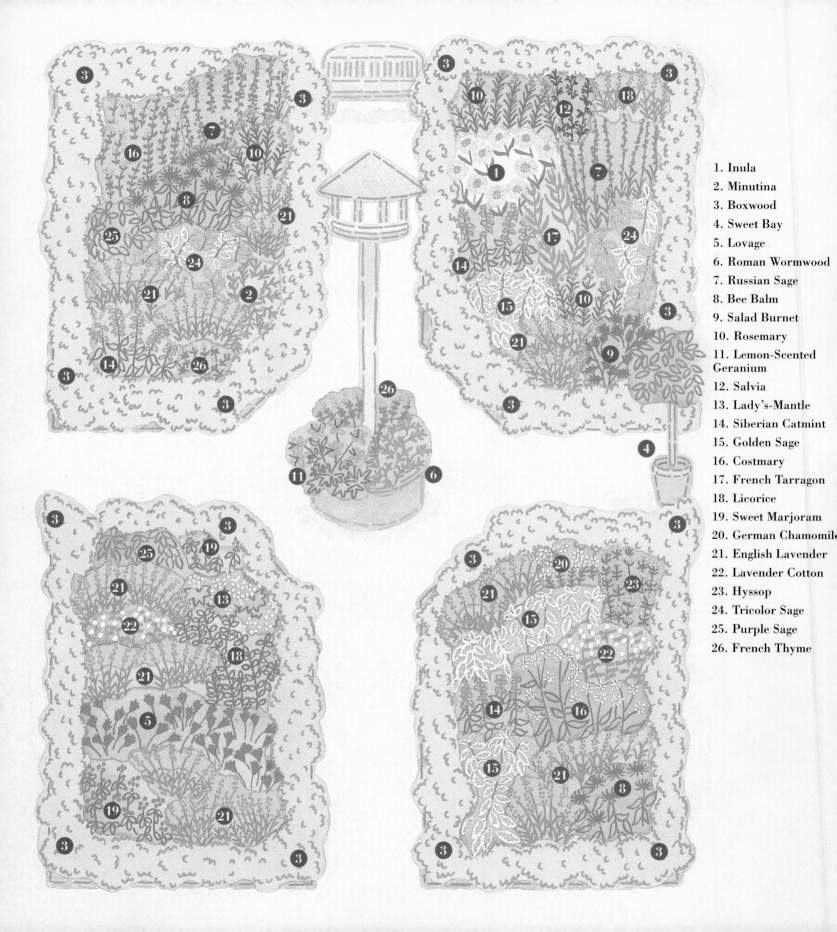

1. Inula
2. Minutina
3. Boxwood
4. Sweet Bay
5. Lovage
6. Roman Wormwood
7. Russian Sage
8. Bee Balm
9. Salad Burnet
10. Rosemary
11. Lemon-Scented Geranium
12. Salvia
13. Lady's-Mantle
14. Siberian Catmint
15. Golden Sage
16. Costmary
17. French Tarragon
18. Licorice
19. Sweet Marjoram
20. German Chamomile
21. English Lavender
22. Lavender Cotton
23. Hyssop
24. Tricolor Sage
25. Purple Sage
26. French Thyme

minutina

Plantago coronopus
- Annual
- Summer
- 6"
- 50 days
- Foliage plant
- Sun
- Sources: h, w

Also known as buck's-horn plantain. Cold-hardy, cut-and-come-again salad green. Broadcast seeds. Harvest in spring or fall.

inula

Inula spp.
- Perennial, subshrub
- 8–9'
- Summer
- Yellow, yellow-orange
- Zones 3–8
- Sun

- Sources: f, n

Large, daisy-like flowers. Height varies with species. Some require more water than others. Grows in ordinary, well-drained soil. Excellent as cut flowers. Attracts butterflies. Divide every 3–8 years.

boxwood

Buxus microphylla var. *koreana*
- Evergreen shrub
- 24–30", spread to 5'
- Foliage plant
- Shiny, green leaves
- Zones 4–9
- Sun or shade
- Source: j

Low, rounded shrub; slow-growing. Very hardy; will survive where other boxwoods may freeze. Mulch with leaf mold; protect from drying winds.

sweet bay

Laurus nobilis
- Evergreen tree or shrub
- 12"–40'
- Spring
- Yellow
- Aromatic foliage
- Zones 8–10

- Sun, partial shade
- Sources: n, hh, vv

True, culinary bay leaf. Tolerates being pruned into desired shapes; used for topiaries, standards, and hedges.

lovage

Levisticum officinale
- Perennial, herb
- 2–6'
- Summer
- Greenish yellow
- Zones 3–8
- Sun
- Sources: u, w, ee, ii, aaa

Large plant grown for its leaves, stems, and seeds, which smell and taste like celery. Easier to grow than celery. Great flavoring with potatoes.

roman wormwood

Artemisia pontica
- Perennial
- 4'
- Summer
- Whitish yellow
- Zones 4–8
- Sun
- Source: oo

Small, fern-like, silver leaves. Wormwood prefers light, well-drained soil. Great in borders, rock gardens. Used in sachets.

russian sage

Perovskia atriplicifolia
- Perennial
- 3–4', spreads to 4'
- Summer to early fall
- Soft blue

- Aromatic foliage
- Zones 3–9
- Sun
- Sources: ee, eee, jjj

Numerous stems of gray-green foliage. Not finicky about soil type, but must be well-drained. Heat- and drought-resistant; can take humidity, too. Cut back in early spring.

bee balm

Monarda didyma
'Cambridge Scarlet'
- Perennial
- 2–5'
- Summer
- Bright red
- Zones 4–9
- Sun
- Sources: c, n, eee, iii

A popular old variety of an eastern U.S. native. Deadhead to keep blooms coming. Needs moist soil and good air circulation. Spreads quickly.

rosemary

Rosmarinus officinalis
'Tuscan Blue'
- Shrub, evergreen
- 6' tall, 4' spread
- Winter, spring
- Fragrant
- Blue-violet
- Zones 8–10
- Sun, partial sun
- Sources: n, s, iii, fff

Likes rich, well-drained soil. Edible flowers with milder flavor than the leaves; add them to a tossed salad.

salad burnet

Sanguisorba minor
(*Poterium sanguisorba*)
- Perennial, herb
- 18–24"
- Summer
- Dusky pink
- Zones 3–8
- Sun, light shade
- Sources: f, n, w, oo

Salad herb with mild cucumber flavor. Use young leaves and flowers in salads, vinegars. Cut back for steady supply of fresh leaves for the kitchen.

lemon-scented geranium

Pelargonium graveolens
'Rober's Lemon Rose'
- Perennial, subshrub
- 3'
- Spring, summer
- Lemon-rose scent
- Pink
- Zones 9–10
- Sun
- Sources: n, z, oo, fff

Fuzzy, gray-green leaves. Likes warm, dry days and cool nights.

salvia

Salvia guaranitica
- Perennial, subshrub
- 4', spreads to 5'
- Summer, fall
- Dark blue
- Zones 8–10
- Sun, partial shade
- Source: n

Bushy plant with 2" flowers on 10" spikes. Can be grown as an annual in cold climates. Attracts hummingbirds.

siberian catmint

Nepeta sibirica
- Perennial
- 2–3'
- Spring through fall
- Purplish blue
- Zones 3–8
- Sun
- Sources: iii, jjj

Gray-green leaves. Blooms profusely with 10" spikes of flowers. Tolerant of moisture; needs well-drained soil.

lady's-mantle

Alchemilla mollis
- Perennial
- 3'
- Summer
- Yellow
- Zones 3–7
- Sun, partial shade
- Sources: f, eee, jjj

Ornamental, light green foliage blanketed with flowers. Good for low borders, rock gardens, groundcovers, draping over a low wall. Excellent for cut or dried flowers.

golden sage

Salvia officinalis 'Aurea'
- Perennial, shrub
- 12"
- Summer
- Foliage plant—yellow and green leaves
- Aromatic foliage
- Zones 7–8
- Sun, light shade
- Source: oo

A culinary sage grown for its attractive yellow and green leaves. Sage prefers light, well-drained soil.

french tarragon

Artemisia dracunculus
- Perennial, herb
- 2–3'
- Summer
- Greenish white flowers
- Aromatic foliage
- Zones 4–9
- Sun, partial shade
- Sources: h, ii, oo, fff

Don't confuse with Russian tarragon, which is inferior in flavor.

costmary

Tanacetum balsamita
(*Chrysanthemum balsamita*)
- Perennial, herb
- 12–36"
- Late summer, fall
- White

- Aromatic leaves
- Zones 6–8
- Sun, partial shade
- Source: oo

The minty leaves are traditionally used as bookmarks. Use young leaves in drinks and green or fruit salads. Spreads aboveground, so don't mulch around the plant.

licorice

Glycyrrhiza glabra
- Perennial, herb
- 3'
- Summer
- Purple, blue
- Zones 9–10
- Sun, partial shade
- Source: aaa

A legume, it has pea-like flowers. Likes rich, moist soil, neutral pH. Caution: should not be used by people with heart, kidney, or obesity problems or by pregnant women.

sweet marjoram

Origanum marjorana
- Perennial, herb
- 12"
- Late summer, fall
- White or pink
- Zones 8–10

- Spring–midsummer
- Sun
- Sources: h, w, ii, oo, aaa, fff

Grow as an annual in zones 7 and below, or in hot, humid areas. Does well in containers. Both the leaves and edible flowers are used in cooking.

german chamomile

Matricaria recutita
- Annual, herb
- 6–24"
- Summer
- Fragrant
- White
- Sun, partial shade
- Sources: w, ff, uu

Better flavor than perennial chamomile. Good for tea. Flowers have an apple scent. Reseeds.

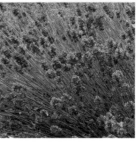

english lavender

Lavandula angustifolia
(*L. officinalis*) 'Hidcote'
- Evergreen shrub, herb
- 15–20"
- Summer
- Fragrant
- Rich, deep purple
- Sun
- Zones 5–10
- Sources: oo, aaa, eee, jjj

Grows well in cool, drier areas of Zones 8–10, but not in hot, humid areas— grow there as annuals in fast-draining containers.

lavender cotton

Santolina pinnata ssp. *neapolitana* hyb.
(*S. neapolitana* hyb.)
- Evergreen shrub
- 30"

- Summer
- Bright yellow
- Aromatic foliage
- Zones 7–10
- Sun
- Sources: c, oo, iii

Lacy, silvery leaves; button-like flowers. This drought-tolerant plant requires well-drained soil. Use the flowers in dried arrangements.

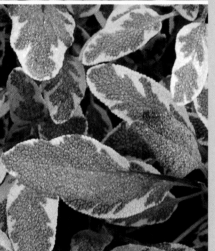

hyssop

Hyssopus officinalis
- Evergreen, herb
- 1–2′
- Summer to fall
- Blue, pink
- Aromatic foliage
- Zones 6–9
- Sun, partial shade
- Sources: h, oo, aaa, fff

Easy to grow. Cut back often to 6″ to keep blooming and bushy. Feed with fish emulsion after cutting back. Leaves and flowers have a quinine flavor.

purple sage

Salvia officinalis 'Purpurascens'
- Perennial, shrub
- 18–24″
- Summer
- Foliage plant—red-purple leaves
- Zones 4–9
- Sun
- Sources: n, oo, iii, fff

For culinary and ornamental use. Start from seeds, cuttings, or divisions, Grow in well-drained soil. Cut back in spring.

tricolor sage

Salvia officinalis 'Tricolor'
- Perennial, shrub
- 18″
- Summer
- Lilac blue
- Foliage plant—pink, green and cream-colored leaves
- Zones 7–10
- Sun, light shade
- Sources: n, oo, fff

Culinary sage grown for its attractive leaves. Mulch in the winter. Treat as an annual in hot, humid climates.

french thyme

Thymus vulgaris 'French'
- Perennial, herb
- 2′
- Summer
- White
- Zones 5–9
- Sun
- Source: fff

Upright-growing, with narrow gray leaves. Has a sweeter fragrance than English thyme. Requires alkaline, well-drained soil. Flavor is fuller when grown in poor soil.

rustic

garden

agarden's setting helps determine its style. This slice of

paradise is a modest complement to the majestic

backdrop of New York's Catskill Mountains. Flowers

and vegetables grow in rustic glory. Mixed plantings

are set in a simple design—a

mere nod to formality—that

allows for experimentation

and change. A handmade

fence frames the picture-

perfect, albeit rustic, scene.

The twig fence sets
the tone of the
garden and serves
to keep rabbits out
of the vegetables.
Opposite: Cleome.

the layout of Dean Riddle's New York garden is simple: Plants grow in four rectangles, each of which is lopped off at the inner corner to echo the curve of a

anchored by a boxwood ball plopped in the outer corner like an evergreen paperweight. For consistency, purple cabbage contrasts with lettuce along the curves of all four beds.

Gray stones that emerged during tilling or lay waiting in the soothing waters of a

hydrangeas, and asters, as well as zebra grass, which looks equally lovely in winter.

Perhaps it is Dean's garden fence that goes the farthest in making a

quickly became his tree of preference for the project, as its wood is straight, workable, and durable. He trimmed each picket by hand for an undulating fence top and attached hardware cloth from the lower rail down to the ground to deter hungry rabbits.

CHANGING BEDS

Dean achieves a fairly informal look by planting mixed borders in the front and rear beds, and annuals in the outer quadrants. The quads change in composition each year, allowing for some experimentation. This is important in all gardens, but especially so in small ones.

a small garden with a big impact

central circle. The beds lie separated by swept earthen paths, just far enough apart to allow access from all sides for easy sowing, weeding, and harvesting. Beyond the small, fenced-in 22×30-foot plot rise the Catskills, a background so majestic that only a modest design could complement it.

Each bed contains a different mixture of vegetables and flowers, a strategy that enables Dean to raise a variety of favorites. Leafy crops such as kohlrabi, beets, and lettuces grow neatly in tightly combed rows. Each quadrant is

nearby creek now edge the planting areas. The tidy lines of stone raise the beds several inches to hold well-worked soil enriched with generous helpings of manure.

Outer beds tucked along the garden's edge provide room for a chorus of summer plantings, including sunflowers, Joe-Pye weed, snakeroot, cleome, dahlias, zinnias, and red orach. For fall splendor, Dean includes showy stonecrop, peegee

rustic statement. No ordinary picket fence would suffice in such a setting. After two months spent collecting more than 500 hardwood saplings, Dean attached green stick pickets to pine rails and posts using galvanized finishing nails driven at an angle. Ash

Inside the fence, blossoms and crops flourish through the seasons, from tulips and lettuce to zinnias and bush beans. Planted in plots carved from the earth by man, a garden of native materials grows at home with natural beauty that sprawls around it.

For contrast, the inner beds have geometric rows. In key places, particular plants are used to accent formality. Tulips color the garden in spring, planted in small drifts among shrubs and perennials and in neat clusters along the main path.

Annuals fill gaps later as spring moves into summer. Nasturtiums, marigolds, and globe amaranth replace early vegetables. Scattered patches of salad leaves grow in small openings at the base of larger plants.

Favorite plants are allowed to self-sow. Happy volunteers of flowering tobacco and red orach rise through neighboring annuals and bring spirit to the garden with their natural, carefree habits.

Lettuces and violas make a beautiful mix—in the garden or in a salad. *Opposite:* Overview of the garden.

For years Dean Riddle *dreamed* about a garden of his

own, storing ideas from others he studied. When he purchased his dream property in the Catskill Mountains, he immediately worked to achieve his goal—a kitchen garden with simple and rustic charm and touches of elegance. There is a bit of magic that comes from melding plants with design. Today, the garden continues to flourish due to Dean's persistent experimentation—discovering another heirloom flower or vegetable that he must try in the garden. And that is the greatest lesson of all—a well-made garden, however small, can offer years of pleasure through refining its style.

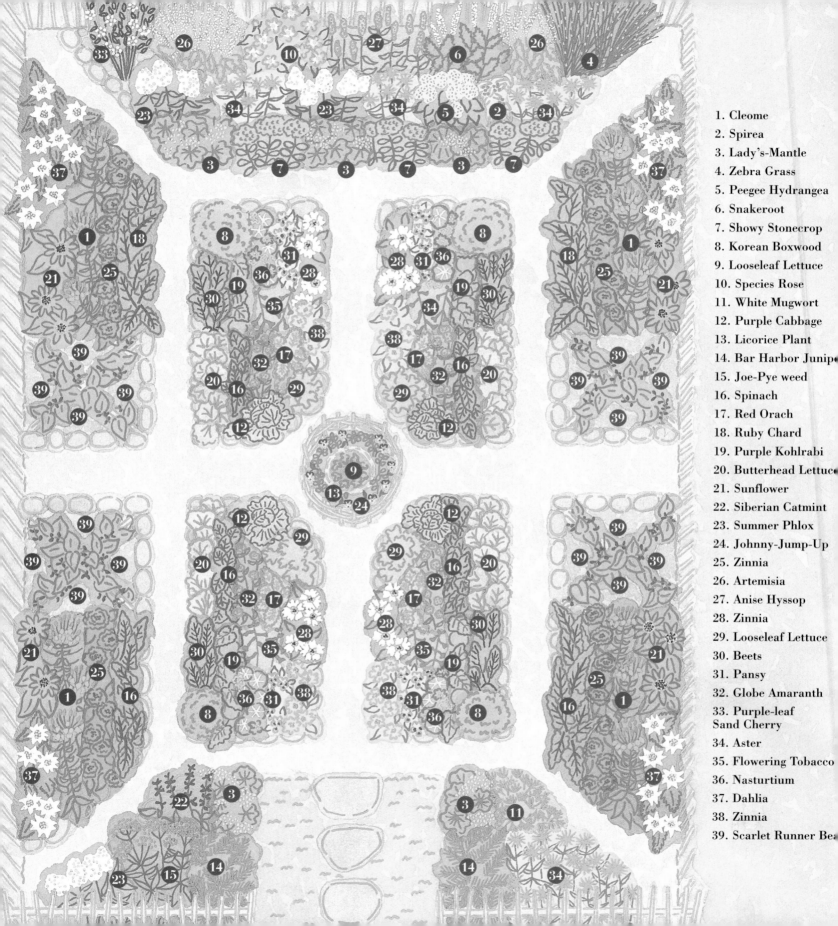

1. Cleome
2. Spirea
3. Lady's-Mantle
4. Zebra Grass
5. Peegee Hydrangea
6. Snakeroot
7. Showy Stonecrop
8. Korean Boxwood
9. Looseleaf Lettuce
10. Species Rose
11. White Mugwort
12. Purple Cabbage
13. Licorice Plant
14. Bar Harbor Juniper
15. Joe-Pye weed
16. Spinach
17. Red Orach
18. Ruby Chard
19. Purple Kohlrabi
20. Butterhead Lettuce
21. Sunflower
22. Siberian Catmint
23. Summer Phlox
24. Johnny-Jump-Up
25. Zinnia
26. Artemisia
27. Anise Hyssop
28. Zinnia
29. Looseleaf Lettuce
30. Beets
31. Pansy
32. Globe Amaranth
33. Purple-leaf
Sand Cherry
34. Aster
35. Flowering Tobacco
36. Nasturtium
37. Dahlia
38. Zinnia
39. Scarlet Runner Bean

cleome

Cleome hassleriana 'Violet Queen'
- Annual
- 4–6'
- Summer to fall
- Purple
- Sun, partial shade
- Sources: e, u, ii, kk, tt

Also know as spider flower. Attracts hummingbirds. Sow in early spring or fall. Great for back of the border.

spirea

Spiraea japonica (*S. bumalda*) 'Goldflame'
- Deciduous shrub
- 3–5'
- Summer
- Dark pink
- Zones 4–8
- Sun, light shade
- Sources: l, t, eee

Leaves are bronze-tinted when young, yellow in the summer, and copper-orange in the fall. Deadheading the spent flower clusters encourages a second blooming.

lady's-mantle

Alchemilla mollis
- Perennial
- 1–3'
- Summer
- Yellow-green
- Zones 3–7

- Sun, partial shade
- Sources: f, i, eee, jjj

Scalloped leaves catch and hold morning dew. The multitudes of small flowers put on a long show. Grow in partial shade in hot-summer climates.

zebra grass

Miscanthus sinensis 'Zebrinus'
- Perennial, ornamental grass
- 6–8'
- Early fall
- Reddish
- Zones 6–9
- Sun
- Sources: c, l, t, eee

Light green leaves with horizontal bands of yellow. Does best in moist, well-drained, fertile soil.

peegee hydrangea

Hydrangea paniculata 'Grandiflora'
- Deciduous shrub, small tree
- 10–15' as shrub, to 25' for tree
- Summer, fall
- White turning pink-red
- Zones 3–8
- Sun, partial shade
- Sources: e, ggg

Flowers are in long clusters. Leaves turn pink-bronze in the fall. Fast-growing; prune to shape after blooming.

snakeroot

Actaea racemosa (*Cimicifuga racemosa*)
- Perennial
- 4–6'
- Summer, fragrant
- White
- Zones 3–10
- Part shade, sun

- Sources: oo, jjj

Native plant with handsome, divided, dark green leaves. Tall, wiry stems. Attractive late-summer racemes of flowers look like fairy wands. Good plant for an evening garden.

showy stonecrop

Hylotelephium (*Sedum*) 'Autumn Joy'
- Perennial
- 24–30"
- Late summer, early fall
- Pink to rose
- Zones 3–9
- Sun
- Sources: c, i, jjj

Neat, succulent foliage and long-lasting blooms.

korean boxwood

Buxus microphylla var. *koreana* 'Winter Gem'
- Shrub, evergreen
- 24"
- Foliage plant
- Zones 4–9
- Sun or shade
- Source: l

One of the hardiest of the boxwoods. Compact plant with dark green leaves; good color all through winter.

looseleaf lettuce

Lactuca sativa
'Red Sails'
- Annual
- 12" across
- 45–60 days
- Spring to fall
- Sun
- Sources: h, w, ii, zz, aaa

Beautiful loose heads of ruffled leaves; green overlaid with burgundy red. Fast-growing and slow to bolt. Grow for baby lettuce or grow on to maturity.

species rose

Rosa glauca
(*R. rubrifolia*)
- Shrub, deciduous
- 6'
- Late spring–early summer
- Pink
- Zones 2–8
- Sun
- Sources: b, g, l, jjj

Distinctive grayish purple foliage. Small single blossoms are in clusters. Many red-orange hips in the fall.

white mugwort

Artemisia ludoviciana
'Valerie Finnis'
- Perennial
- 4–5'
- Late summer–midfall

- Creamy white
- Zones 5–8
- Sun
- Source: v

Lovely fern-like leaves. The species is different than most artemisias, as the flowers are attractive and the leaves are dark green. Artemisias need moderate water, good drainage.

purple cabbage

Brassica oleracea
Capitata group
- Biennial grown as annual
- 2–7 pounds
- 70–90 days
- Purple to purple-red
- Spring, fall
- Sun or light shade
- Sources: h, q, ii, vv, zz

A cool-season crop; gets bitter-tasting if grown during hot weather.

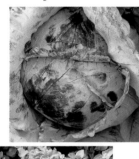

licorice plant

Helichrysum petiolare
'Limelight'
- Shrub, evergreen
- 3'
- Late summer, fall, winter
- White
- Zones 8–10
- Sun
- Source: i

Small, lime green leaves. The species has woolly, gray leaves. Often grown as an annual. Needs well-drained, poor to medium soil.

bar harbor juniper

Juniperus horizontalis
'Bar Harbor'
- Evergreen shrub
- 2', 10–12' spread
- Foliage plant
- Zones 4–9
- Sun
- Source: bb

Good groundcover plant. Blue-green to light green needles. Tough; grows in most soils, as long as well-drained. Salt-tolerant; good for seaside gardens.

joe-pye weed

Eupatorium maculatum
'Gateway'
- Perennial
- 4'
- Summer
- Dusky purple
- Zones
- Sun, light shade
- Sources: c, i

Wine red stems. Easy to grow. Native American plant. Not a weed, despite its name. Attracts butterflies.

spinach

Spinacia oleracea
- Annual
- 6"
- 35–45 days to harvest
- Spring, fall
- Dark green foliage
- Sun
- Sources: h, w, ff, uu

Cool-season plant. Likes a rich, evenly moist soil with good drainage. Make successive, small sowings to keep a fresh crop coming. Nutritious; great in salads or cooked.

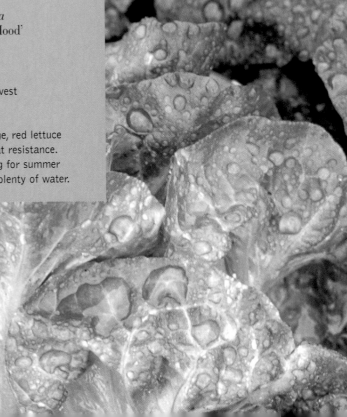

red orach

Atriplex hortensis
- Annual
- To 6', seed spikes
- 37–40 days
- Spring, summer
- Red foliage
- Sun
- Sources: m, w

Plant this salad green in early spring. Pinch back the plants to keep them producing into summer or otherwise they will go to seed.

purple kohlrabi

Brassica oleracea
Gongylodes Group
- Biennial grown as annual
- 38–60 days
- Spring–fall harvest in North, fall–winter in South
- Grown for stem
- Sun
- Sources: w, ff, ii, uu, zz, aaa

Grown for the purple bulb-like portion of the stem right above the soil level. Prefers cool weather. Has crunchy, sweet flesh; can be eaten raw.

ruby chard

Beta vulgaris
'Ruby Red' ('Rhubarb')
- Grown as annual
- 24"
- 59 days
- Spring to fall harvest
- Red stalks and leaf veins
- Sun
- Sources: q, w, uu

Rich, ruby red stalks and dark green leaves are glorious in the garden and tasty on the dinner plate. An heirloom vegetable, grown for years.

butterhead lettuce

Lactuca sativa
'Red Riding Hood'
- Annual
- 6–8"
- 60–75 days
- Summer harvest
- Sun
- Source: h

Beautiful, large, red lettuce with great heat resistance. Plant in spring for summer harvest. Give plenty of water.

sunflower

Helianthus annuus
'Red Sun'
- Annual
- 6'
- Summer, fall
- Deep red
- Sun
- Source: u

Velvety red flowers with brown center. Great cut flowers. Easy to grow; sow where you want them to grow; heat- and drought-resistant.

summer phlox

Phlox paniculata
'Mt. Fuji' ('Fujiyama')
- 26"
- Summer–early fall
- Fragrant
- White
- Zones 3–8
- Sun
- Source: eee

Sweetly-scented, old-fashioned flowers. Needs good air circulation to prevent mildew. Deadhead to keep plant from self-sowing.

siberian catmint

Nepeta sibirica 'Blue Beauty'
('Souvenir d'Andre Chaudron')
- Perennial
- 18"
- Spring through fall
- Purplish blue
- Zones 3–8
- Sun
- Source: i

Larger flowers than the species. Cut back before flowering, to keep plant compact.

johnny-jump-up

Viola tricolor
- Perennial grown as annual
- 6–12"
- Spring, summer
- Purple, yellow, and white
- Sun, shade
- Zones 4–10
- Sources: w, ii

Favorite for interplanting among daffodils and tulips in spring. Self-sows. Edible flowers. Thrives in cool weather.

zinnia

Zinnia angustifolia
'White Star'
- Annual
- 14–16"
- Summer–fall
- White, single
- Sun
- Source: uu

Produces a profusion of 2" flowers. Heat-, humidity-, drought-, and disease-resistant plants.

anise hyssop

Agastache foeniculum
- Perennial
- 3–5'
- Summer
- Blue
- Zones 6–10
- Sun
- Sources: h, vv, fff

Tall plant with anise-scented leaves and 4" spikes of flowers. Needs well-drained soil. Good in borders or herb beds. Reseeds.

artemisia

Artemisia ludoviciana
'Powis Castle'
- Perennial
- 2–3' tall, wide-spreading
- Flowers insignificant
- Aromatic, silvery foliage
- Zones 4–8
- Sun
- Sources: f, eee, fff, ggg, jjj

Takes humid heat better than most artemisias. Perfect for white gardens; sets off bright-colored flowers beautifully. Divide in spring or fall.

zinnia

Zinnia elegans
'Scarlet Splendor'
- Annual
- 22"
- Summer
- Scarlet red
- Sun
- Sources: e, uu

Vivid, semiruffled flowers with long stems on bushy, compact plants. Great cut flowers. Heat- and drought-tolerant.

looseleaf lettuce

Lactuca sativa
'Salad Bowl'
- Annual
- 1' across
- 45–60 days
- Harvest spring to fall

- Sun
- Source: h, w, zz, aaa

Deeply lobed, lime-green leaves with excellent flavor. Resistant to bolting. A good cut-and-come-again lettuce—harvest when 4–6" tall, by cutting 1–2" above the crown with scissors; it will regrow.

beets

Beta vulgaris
'Chioggia' & 'Golden'
- Biennial grown as annual
- Roots 2" across
- 50 days
- Harvest spring or fall
- Red beet with white stripes; golden yellow beet
- Sun
- Sources: h, uu, xx

Both are sweet-flavored. 'Chioggia' is an heirloom.

pansy

Viola × wittrockiana
'Antique Shades'
- Perennial grown as annual
- 6–9"
- Spring, early summer
- Soft pastel shades
- Sun, partial shade
- Source: bbb

Elegant pansy in a variety of soft shades that change as they mature. Prefers cool weather, moist, rich soil. Fall-planted pansies overwinter in many areas. Edible flowers with a slightly minty flavor.

globe amaranth

Gomphrena globosa
- Annual
- 12–24"
- Summer to fall
- Pink, purple, red, white
- Sun

- Sources: uu, bbb

Distinctive 1½" round or oval flower heads on ends of stems. Good for cut or dried flowers. Needs moderate water, well-drained soil.

aster

Aster spp.
- Perennial
- 6"–6'
- Late summer–early fall
- Variety of colors with yellow centers
- Zones vary with species
- Full sun usually
- Sources: e, ee, ii, zz, bbb

More than 600 species of true asters and multitudes of cultivars—all with daisy-like flower heads of various sizes. Prefers fertile soil. Tends to be quite cold-hardy.

purple-leaf sand cherry

Prunus × cistena
- Shrub, deciduous
- 5–10' tall
- Spring
- White to light pink
- Zones 4–8
- Sun
- Sources: Local nurseries

Slow-growing; can be trained as a small tree. Attractive red-purple foliage; sometimes bears cherry-like purple fruit.

flowering tobacco

Nicotiana langsdorffii
- Annual
- 3–5'
- Summer

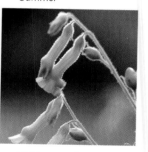

- Light green flowers
- Sun
- Source: bbb

Unusual nicotiana, with branching stems and green flowers. Great conversation starter in a cut-flower bouquet. Unlike other flowering tobaccos, this one isn't fragrant.

nasturtium

Tropaeolum majus
'Alaska'
- Annual
- 1'
- Spring to fall
- Yellow, coral, dark red
- Sun, partial shade
- Sources: ff, ii, tt, uu, bbb

Leaves are marbled cream and green. Direct sow, as nasturtiums don't like to be transplanted. Provide some afternoon shade in hot-summer climates.

zinnia

Zinnia angustifolia
'Gold Star'
- Annual
- 14–16"
- Summer to fall
- Gold, single
- Sun
- Source: uu

Sow in the garden, or start inside and transplant; flowers in 6 weeks from seed. Blooms happily all season with little care. Good container plant.

dahlia

Dahlia 'Mignon Silver'
- Perennial, tuber
- Late summer, fall
- 15–20"
- White
- Zones 8–10
- Sun
- Source: bbb

Single flowers, 2" or less. Dahlias thrive in Pacific Coast climate. In zones 7 and colder, at first frost cut back to 6" and lift the tubers and store indoors for winter.

scarlet runner bean

Phaseolus coccineus
- Perennial grown as annual, vine
- 6–8'
- Summer
- Red
- Zones
- Sun
- Sources: w, ff, uu, aaa, ddd

Long, meaty green pods and edible scarlet flowers. Perennial in mild-winter climates.

four-season garden

A grape-covered pergola is cool in summer and is visually interesting in winter. *Opposite:* Egyptian onion.

a

ny garden can be captivating in summer. But to delight the eye in winter, when nothing is in bloom and the landscape is frozen, it demands special attention. Strong focal points in the hardscape— a pergola, trellises, wattle fences, garden troughs, sinks, architectural capitals, iron benches, and bistro tables— anchor this Missouri garden, making it a year-round pleasure. During the growing season, the plants are the star attractions. And in the snow, it's a magical delight.

artists Bruce Burstert and Robert Raymond Smith enjoy their Kansas City garden year-round. "Lots of people think in terms of gardens from April 1st to October 1st," says Bruce. "We want something going on all the time."

The garden's appeal begins in the dead of winter. A stark black pergola, devoid of foliage, dominates the setting, its architectural bones as prominent in the barren season as sculpture. Texture rules during cold months. Wattle fences show off their woven forms against the frozen landscape. Snow-dusted shapes of trimmed conifer hedges frame the garden with plump silhouettes.

But when spring arrives, color steals into the scene. Bulbs bring the first flush as jonquils, narcissus, and tulips uncurl from winter naps. Tiny, new leaves appear, and blossoms wreath the garden at all levels, from a carpet of violets underfoot to dogwood branches overhead.

Summer finds food crops mixed in with the ornamentals—not just in the kitchen garden but throughout the property. Espaliered apples— 'Jonafree' and 'Liberty' selections—hug the arbor, while scarlet runner beans fill the rest of the frame with foliage. A low, clipped hedge of germander divides the central rectangle of the kitchen garden into crisp triangles and diamonds. Other beds are filled with chives, dianthus, verbena, yarrow, bourbon roses, and common thrift. Thick rows of kale and 'Ruby' Swiss chard border other beds with beauty good enough to eat. The chards are especially lovely planted where the early morning or late afternoon sun can illuminate the colorful ribs, making them glow like jewels. Gooseberry bushes substitute for privacy fencing.

Apples ripen in autumn as bean pods deepen to purple, bringing color to the arbor. Asters and anemones take over where summer flowers left off; seed heads and browning foliage begin the shift in interest from color back to texture again. Bruce fashions whimsical figures from wire and straw—people, peacocks, and chickens —to tuck into empty corners. Frost falls, then snow, and the garden begins another year.

creating year-round **visual** interest

A vine circle is all but hidden by the clematis, but in winter it stands out. *Opposite:* Overview of the garden.

WATTLE FENCES

Wattle fences are traditionally made in the spring, using the prunings from winter cleanup. They are easy to make, using cut saplings or strong twigs for the supports, and vines (long, supple twigs or branches work well, too—willow is best) to weave the fence. You can make a short wattle fence as an edging or one up to six feet tall as a border.

Pound a sapling into the ground every 12 inches where you want the fence to be. The higher the fence, the stronger the supports need to be. Starting at ground level, weave the vine—alternating in front and behind the supports. Insert new pieces of vine behind a support as needed and continue weaving. A tight weave produces a stronger fence, but a loose weave gives a less formal appearance. Weave the wattle to about 8 to 12 inches from the top of the supports.

As a finishing touch, arch pieces of vine between the supports for a scalloped effect on the top of the fence.

Visitors to this **all-season** garden must be surprised to learn that this is the first horticultural effort on the part of Bruce Burstert and Robert Raymond Smith. These Kansas City artists and antiques dealers both have families who gardened, but neither of them had previously been involved with the land. Before they started, they researched the subject. Two major influences are British writers Gertrude Jekyll, who popularized informal drifts of plants, and Rosemary Verey, whose writing shaped their approach to year-round gardening. Nonetheless, the greatest influence on Robert and Bruce's garden is their commitment to its ongoing beauty.

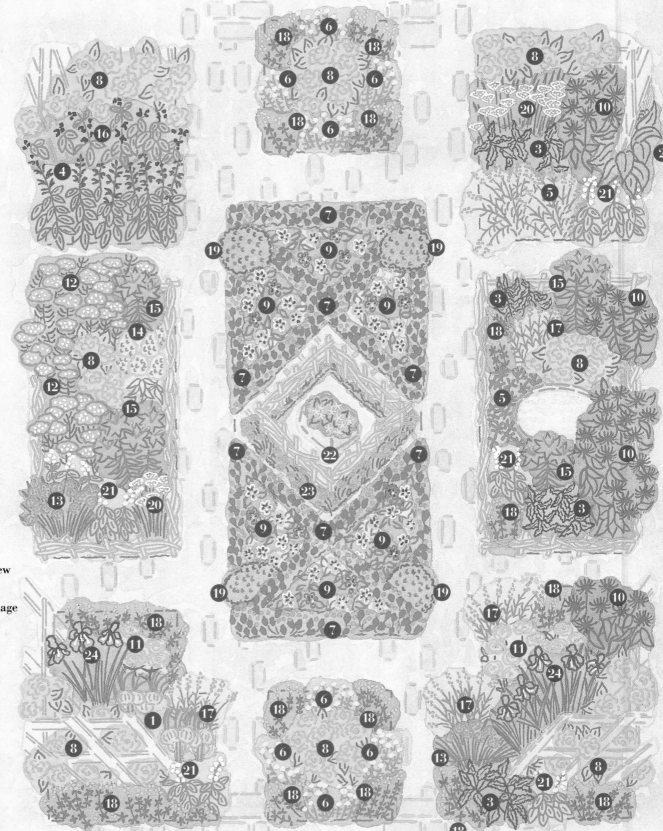

1. Egyptian Onion
2. Elecampane
3. Purple Basil
4. Pineapple Sage
5. Rue
6. Lavender Cotton
7. Germander
8. Floribunda Rose
9. Pansy
10. Bee Balm
11. Calendula
12. Yarrow
13. Chives
14. Summer Phlox
15. Asiatic Lily
16. Gentian Sage
17. Dwarf English Lavender
18. Orange Balsam Thyme
19. Dwarf Weeping Yew
20. Garlic Chives
21. White-Flowered Sage
22. Sedum
23. Common Thrift
24. Blue Flag

elecampane

Inula helenium
- Perennial, subshrub
- To 9' tall, 3' wide
- Summer
- Yellow
- Zones 3–8
- Sun, partial shade
- Source: n

Large plant with basal rosettes of leaves up to 32" long. Spreads by rhizomes. Likes moist but well-drained soil.

egyptian onion

Allium cepa
Proliferum Group
- Perennial, bulb
- 20–36"
- Spring to fall

- 120 days (spring-planted), 250 days (fall-planted)
- Zones 5–8
- Sun
- Sources: ff, pp, rr

Looks like modern sculpture in the garden. Prefers cool weather. Use as you would scallions; the bulblets are great pickled.

purple basil

Ocimum basilicum
'Purple Ruffles'
- Annual, herb
- 24"
- Summer, early fall
- Lavender-pink
- Aromatic foliage
- Sun
- Sources: h, w, kk, uu, xx

Dark purple, ruffled leaves. Thin seedlings to select for the most colorful plants. Beautiful in a pot mixed with pink flowers. Like all basils, it needs warm weather.

pineapple sage

Salvia elegans
- Perennial, herb
- To 6'
- Late summer, fall, winter (in frost-free areas)
- Bright red

- Zones 8–10
- Sun
- Sources: e, n, oo, fff

The medium green, sweet-scented leaves are a pleasure in the garden. Fast-growing. Needs well-drained soil. The edible flowers attract hummingbirds.

rue

Ruta graveolens
- Perennial
- 2–3'
- Summer
- Yellow
- Zones 5–9
- Sun
- Sources: n, oo, fff

Attractive blue-green, fern-like leaves. Needs fertile soil; add lime if soil is very acidic. Use the brown seed capsules in dried flower arrangements.

lavender cotton

Santolina rosmarinifolia
(*S. virens*)
- Evergreen shrub
- 2'
- Summer
- Yellow
- Aromatic foliage
- Zones 6–9
- Sun
- Sources: oo, eee, fff

Not good in the hot, humid South. Mounding green foliage, covered by button-like flowers. Needs well-drained soil.

germander

Teucrium chamaedrys
- Evergreen perennial
- 1' high, 2' wide
- Summer to fall
- Pink to magenta, white

- Zones 5–9
- Sun
- Sources: c, f, eee

Tough plant. Likes moist, well-drained soil; cannot tolerate soggy soil. Use as a low hedge or ground cover for small spaces. Cut back to encourage bushy form. Traditionally used in knot gardens.

floribunda rose

Rosa 'Angel Face'
- Shrub
- 3'
- Spring to fall
- Heady fragrance
- Lavender
- Zones 5–9
- Sun
- Source: g

Edible flowers; handsome dark foliage. Give good air circulation to prevent powdery mildew.

bee balm

Monarda didyma
- Perennial
- To 4'
- Summer
- Aromatic leaves
- Rose red
- Zones 4–9
- Sun
- Sources: c, n

Edible flowers with spicy, sweet flavor. Attracts hummingbirds. Tends to get powdery mildew. Deadhead flowers for rebloom.

pansy

Viola × wittrockiana 'Antique Shades'
- Perennial
- 6–9"
- Spring, early summer
- Soft pastel shades
- Sun, partial shade
- Source: bbb

Gives an old-fashioned air to a garden. Keep flowers picked to encourage blooming. Pansy flowers are edible and have a slight wintergreen taste.

calendula

Calendula officinalis
- Annual
- 1–2'
- Spring, summer
- Yellow, orange
- Sun
- Sources: e, ff, ii, tt, aaa

Also known as pot marigold. Perfect plant for an edible landscape. May reseed. Thrives in cool weather. In the kitchen, use the edible petals to brighten up a salad or sprinkle over soup.

yarrow

Achillea millefolium
- Perennial
- 24″
- Summer–fall
- White, yellow, pink shades
- Zones 3–9
- Sun
- Sources: u, kk, oo, zz, iii

Undemanding plant with fern-like leaves. Needs well-drained soil; drought-tolerant once established. Deadhead spent flower stalks at the base for rebloom.

summer phlox

Phlox paniculata
'Bright Eyes'
- Perennial
- To 4′
- Summer–fall
- Light pink with red centers
- Zones 4–8
- Sun, partial shade
- Sources: c, f, ggg, jjj

Grow in rich, moist soil. Stake if needed. Deadhead to encourage continuous blooms; cut back to the ground in the fall.

chives

Allium schoenoprasum
- Perennial, bulb
- 12–18″
- Early summer
- Lavender
- Zones 3–9
- Sun
- Sources: ii, kk, oo, vv, zz, aaa

Pretty plant that's easy to grow. Leaves and edible flowers (chopped) are delicious with eggs, soups, cheeses, salads, and baked potatoes. Grow from divisions or seeds.

asiatic lily

Lilium hyb.
- Perennial, bulb
- 18–60″
- Summer
- Many colors
- Zones 3–8
- Tops in sun, roots in shade
- Sources: aa, gg, jjj

Lilies like loose, organic soil that stays moist but is not soggy. Don't let the roots dry out. Most need some winter chill and may not perform well in the Deep South.

gentian sage

Salvia patens
- Perennial, subshrub
- 2–3'
- Summer, fall
- True blue
- Zones 8–9
- Sun
- Sources: n, oo, fff

Two-inch-long flowers on erect, branched stems. Needs well-drained soil. Grow as an annual in colder zones.

dwarf english lavender

Lavandula angustifolia 'Nana'
- Shrub
- 12–18"
- Summer
- Fragrant
- Lavender-blue
- Sun
- Zones 5–10
- Source: s

Must have good drainage. Doesn't do well in hot, humid climates.

orange balsam thyme

Thymus vulgaris 'Orange Balsam'
- Perennial, herb
- 6–12"
- Spring, summer
- White to pale pink

- Zones 4–9
- Sun
- Sources: n, oo, fff

Prefers light, dry, well-drained soil. Very tiny, gray-green leaves with unusual orange flavor. Edible flowers. Add a few chopped leaves or flowers to a vinaigrette made with orange juice.

garlic chives

Allium tuberosum
- Perennial, bulb
- 18–30"
- Summer
- White
- Zones 4–8
- Sun
- Sources: ii, kk, vv, zz, aaa

Easy to grow and maintain. Edible flowers. Plant spring through summer in well-drained soil. Divide as needed. Reseeds readily. Cut back severely if it becomes woody.

dwarf weeping yew

Taxus baccata 'Repandens'
- Evergreen shrub
- 24" high, 15' spread
- Foliage plant
- Zones 7–8
- Sun to deep shade
- Source: i

Forms a handsome evergreen mound. Prefers fertile, well-drained soil. Can be pruned but rarely needs it.

white-flowered sage

Salvia officinalis 'Albiflora'
- Perennial, herb
- 2–3'
- Summer
- White
- Aromatic gray-green leaves

- Zones 3–10
- Sun
- Source: n

Soft and soothing in the landscape. A culinary sage which is the same as the species, only with white, edible flowers. Use in the kitchen in the same way. Add flowers to vinegar, sauteed poultry, or pork.

sedum

Sedum kamtschaticum
- Perennial
- 4" tall, 10" wide
- Late summer
- Golden yellow, pink buds
- Zones 4–9
- Sun
- Source: Local nurseries

Glossy, deep green, spoon-shaped leaves sprinkled with star-shaped flowers. Likes moderately rich, well-drained soil.

common thrift

Armeria maritima
- Evergreen perennial
- 8"
- Late spring, summer
- Pink to lavender-pink
- Zones 3–9
- Sun
- Sources: q, kk, iii

For rock gardens, front of border. Takes salt spray and wind but not prolonged heat. Prefers well-drained, poor to medium soil.

blue flag

Iris versicolor
- Perennial, bulb
- 8–32"
- Summer
- Light violet-blue to red-purple
- Zones 3–9
- Sun, partial shade
- Sources: c, f, ee, oo, jjj

Native American iris. Likes moist, acid soil. Will grow in shallow water at pond's edge.

crossed

paths

Crushed shell paths are care-free by day and are quite visible in the evening. *Opposite:* Lamb's ears.

t
he beauty of Evalyn Walch's herb garden is carried by the breeze. Spicy, sweet, and fruity scents mingle like old acquaintances, beckoning from the garden that grows along the salt marshes of Virginia's Eastern Shore. Soft mounds of herbs that gracefully spill over the rigid lines soften the overall appearance. Each area is a rich variation of herb shapes, foliage colors, and textures. Brushing their leaves while walking down any path releases pleasing aromas.

a new garden from the ground up

Where once a thick tangle of briars and honeysuckle grew, an old-fashioned bouquet of herbs and perennials now flourishes. Evalyn and Tony Walch retired to a farm in Virginia, building a house and planting the garden that had grown for years only in Evalyn's mind.

As a designer of herb gardens who lacked the time and space to do any real digging, Evalyn had contented herself for years with developing other people's dreams. But she knew when she saw the fertile, well-drained soil of her new home that the time had come to start a garden of her own.

The Walches built their house first, but Evalyn immediately began visualizing the garden, making notes on scraps of paper. Together with ideas from her past designs and from gardens she had visited, the scribbles turned into sketches and, finally, into a plan. In fact, Evalyn did all her gardening with a pencil before she ever touched a trowel. "It's much easier to move plants around on paper," she explains.

Each plant was purchased with the knowledge of exactly where it would go. Such advance planning made it possible for Evalyn to concentrate on the details of her design. With the skill of a perfumer, she layered aromatic herbs and fragrant flowers for the best mix of scents.

Sweet-smelling roses tumble over trellises, while herbs, such as fennel and lemongrass, stretch to nose level. White clamshell paths border beds of lavender, coriander, and dill; a light swing of the arm or brush of the knee in passing frees the herbs' aromas. Mints growing at a pond's edge can nearly be tasted in the air, growing in a rich assortment of flavors such as apple, chocolate, orange, lemon, and peppermint.

Evalyn also carefully pairs foliage colors, textures, and plant shapes. Some combinations yield eye-catching contrasts, while others form harmonious drifts. Though many herbs are harvested for cooking, Evalyn enjoys collecting the colors of summer from her garden. Blue salvia, yellow strawflower (*Helichrysum bracteatum*), and globe amaranth are favorites that retain much of their flower colors when dried. Sprigs of pungent herbs tucked in her arrangements bring forth memories of seasons past.

PROPAGATING HERBS

Evalyn starts new plants by taking 3- to 5-inch cuttings containing at least three leaf nodes from sideshoots of her herbs. Plastic bags hold fresh cuttings temporarily, preventing moisture loss. Evalyn removes lower leaves from cuttings and dips the cut end in a rooting hormone powder. Next, cuttings are set in pots filled with a mixture of equal parts perlite and vermiculite. Plastic film, lightly covering each pot after initial watering, maintains humidity.

Potted cuttings are left for several weeks in a shady spot. After tugging gently on cuttings to check for roots, Evalyn removes the plastic covering for one week before planting baby plants in individual pots. New top growth indicates that the herbs are ready to be transplanted into the garden.

Globe amaranth (foreground) is excellent as a cut or dried flower. *Opposite:* Overview of the garden.

Evalyn and Tony Walch's **high-spirited** landscape

began with an idea. Evalyn always wanted gardens filled with herbs. She believes they are pretty enough to hold their own alongside any plant. Herbs also are rooted in history, each with its own story. For years, Evalyn grew herbs for a retail nursery and designed herb gardens for clients.

The couple finally had the time for their own garden when they retired and bought a 90-acre farm on Virginia's Eastern Shore. She designed the entire landscape in pencil before ever touching a trowel. The simple pleasure of doing has produced the sweet smell of success.

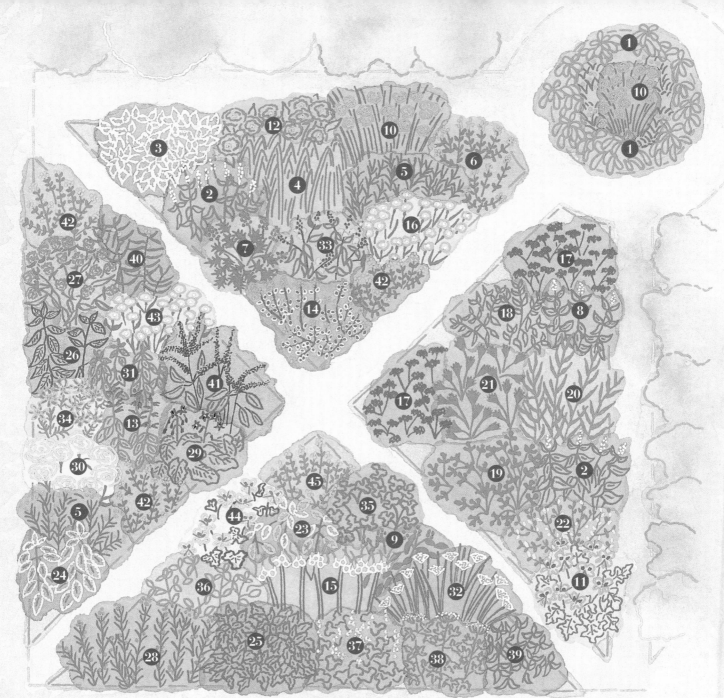

1. Lamb's-Ears
2. Lemon Basil
3. Variegated Oregano
4. Lemongrass
5. Rosemary
6. Thyme
7. Salad Burnet
8. Sweet Basil
9. Sweet Marjoram
10. Chives

11. Scented Geranium
12. Calendula
13. Pineapple Sage
14. Silver Thyme
15. Egyptian Onion
16. Clove Pinks
17. Curly Parsley
18. Globe Basil
19. Italian Broadleaf Parsley

20. French Tarragon
21. Lovage
22. Golden Lemon-Scented Thyme
23. Tricolor Sage
24. Golden Sage
25. Lemon Balm
26. Purple Basil
27. Globe Amaranth
28. Rosemary

29. Borage
30. Tall Marigold
31. Sage
32. Garlic Chives
33. Cinnamon Basil
34. Dwarf Marigold
35. Cilantro/Coriander
36. Golden Oregano
37. French Sorrel
38. Chervil

39. Italian Oregano
40. Summer Savory
41. Grain Amaranth
42. Woolly Thyme
43. Cottage Pinks
44. Lemon-Scented Geranium
45. Lemon Thyme

lemon basil

Ocimum basilicum
'Citriodorum'
(*O. citriodorum* hyb.)
- Annual, herb
- 12–24"
- Summer to fall
- White
- Aromatic foliage
- Sun
- Sources: e, h, ff, ii, oo, fff

There are several cultivars with lemon fragrance. Use leaves and flowers in cooking.

rosemary

Rosmarinus officinalis
'Arp'
- Evergreen shrub
- 4'
- Winter, spring
- Fragrant foliage
- Bright blue
- Zones 7–10
- Sun, partial sun
- Sources: n, s, oo, eee, fff

The hardiest rosemary; can take temperatures down to -10°F. May survive winter in zone 6.

lamb's-ears

Stachys byzantina
(*S. lanata*)
- Perennial
- 3'
- Summer
- White and purple, pink
- Zones 4–9

- Sun
- Sources: c, s, iii

Soft, white, woolly leaves give this plant its name. Needs well-drained soil. Divide and replant the outer part if the plant dies out in the center.

lemongrass

Cymbopogon spp.
- Perennial grass
- 2–3'
- Late summer, early fall
- Grown for foliage
- Sun
- Sources: w, n, oo

Very tender perennial (minimum temperature 50°F). Grow in a pot in most areas or make divisions and bring indoors for the winter. Lemon flavor for teas, curries, soups, desserts.

salad burnet

Sanguisorba minor
(*Poterium sanguisorba*)
- Perennial
- 18–24"
- Summer

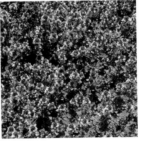

- Dusky pink
- Zones 3–8
- Sun, light shade
- Sources: f, n, w, oo

Attractive plant; can be started from seeds or division. Does well in poor soil. Keep fairly moist. Will reseed. Leaves have a cool cucumber flavor.

variegated oregano

Origanum vulgare
'Variegata' ('Gold Tip')
- Perennial, herb
- 16"
- Spring to early fall
- Aromatic foliage
- Pink or white
- Zones 5–9
- Sun
- Source: oo

Curly leaves yellow at their tips. Low-growing. This oregano tastes like sweet marjoram.

thyme

Thymus vulgaris
- Evergreen perennial, herb
- 6–12"
- Late spring, summer
- Lilac
- Zones 4–9
- Sun
- Sources: n, oo, fff

Also known as common, English, or German thyme. Prefers alkaline, well-drained soil. Likes partial shade in very hot areas. Flavor is fuller when grown in poor soil.

sweet basil

Ocimum basilicum
'Genovese'
- Annual, herb
- 24″
- Summer, early fall
- Aromatic green foliage
- White
- Sun
- Sources: e, h, w, ff, oo, zz
Great, spicy basil flavor; slow
to bolt. Dries well. Put some
in water on a sunny
windowsill; it will root and
live for quite a while.

chives

Allium schoenoprasum
- Perennial, bulb
- 12–18″
- Early summer
- Lavender
- Zones 3–9
- Sun
- Sources: ii, kk, oo, vv, zz, aaa
Chives look best if cut back
occasionally, so harvesting
them is good for the plant.
Use the edible flowers to
make a pale lavender
herb vinegar.

sweet marjoram

Origanum marjoram
- Tender perennial, herb
- 12–24″
- Late summer, fall
- Tiny, white or pink flowers
- Zones 8–10
- Spring–midsummer
- Sun
- Sources: h, w, ii, oo, aaa, fff
Doesn't do well in heat, humidity.
Likes fairly moist, well-drained
soil. Pinch back before it blooms.

scented geranium

Pelargonium quercifolium
'Fair Ellen'
- Perennial, subshrub
- 1–2′
- Spring, summer
- Fragrant
- Light lavender-pink
- Zone 10
- Sun
- Source: n
Leaves have sweet, pungent
scent. Good container plant.

calendula

Calendula officinalis
- Annual
- 1–2'
- Spring, summer
- Yellow, orange
- Sun
- Sources: e, ff, ii, tt, aaa

Easy to grow. Not picky about soil but needs good drainage. The flower petals are edible if not sprayed with pesticide. Chopped petals can be used like saffron in cooking; impart a yellow color.

silver thyme

Thymus × citriodorus 'Argenteus'
- Evergreen perennial, herb
- To 12"
- Summer
- White
- Zones 6–9
- Sun
- Sources: e, n, oo, fff

Upright growth. Silver variegated foliage; gets a pink tinge in cold weather. Leaves and edible flowers have a lemony flavor.

pineapple sage

Salvia elegans
- Perennial, herb
- 6'
- Late summer, fall, winter
- Bright red
- Zones 8–10
- Sun
- Sources: e, n, oo, fff

Wonderful pineapple-scented foliage, spicy-sweet edible flowers—use in drinks or fruit salads. Hummingbirds love the flowers. Pinch back if you want to keep bushy.

egyptian onion

Allium cepa Proliferum Group
- Perennial, bulb
- 20–36"
- Spring to fall
- 120 days (spring-planted), 250 days (fall-planted)
- Zones 5–8
- Sun
- Sources: ff, pp, rr

Order sets in late summer to fall; plant in the fall. You'll have scallions in early spring.

curly parsley

Petroselinum crispum
'Moss Curled'
('Forest Green')
- Biennial grown as annual
- 12"
- 70–85 days
- White flowers 2nd year
- Sun, partial shade
- Sources: q, w, zz, aaa,
Highly curled, dark green
leaves. Makes a lovely
edging plant in the
ground or in a container.

clove pinks

Dianthus caryophyllus
- Perennial
- 18"
- Late spring–summer
- Fragrant
- Pink, white, deep pink
- Zones 6–9

- Sun
- Sources: f, u, ii, zz, iii
Also known as wild
carnation. Single or
double, edible flowers
with a spicy, clove
fragrance. Doesn't like
the humid heat of the
deep South.

italian broadleaf parsley

Petroselinum crispum
var. *neapolitanum*
- Biennial
- 12"
- 75 days

- White flowers 2nd year
- Zones 5–9
- Sun, partial shade
- Sources: w, q, ff, ii
Italian parsley is
considered by many to
be the preferred parsley
for cooking, as it has a
fuller flavor than curly
parsley.

globe basil

Ocimum basilicum
'Spicy Globe'
('Minimum')
- Annual, herb
- 6–14"
- Summer, early fall
- Aromatic green foliage
- White
- Sun
- Sources: w, uu, zz, oo, fff
Also called Greek basil.
Very pretty, round bush
of basil. Perfect for
containers. Use for a
neat garden edging; nice
teamed with 'Lemon
Gem' marigolds.

french tarragon

Artemisia dracunculus
- Perennial, herb
- 2–3'
- Summer
- Greenish white
- Aromatic foliage
- Zone 4–10
- Sun, partial shade
- Sources: h, n, ii, oo, fff
In heat and humidity of
the Deep South, grow it as
a winter annual.

lovage

Levisticum officinale
- Perennial, herb
- 2–6'
- Summer
- Greenish yellow
- Zones 3–9
- Sun, partial shade
- Sources: e, u, w, ii, vv, aaa
Often grown as an
annual in hot, humid
climates. Needs moist
soil, but with good
drainage.

golden lemon-scented thyme

Thymus x citriodorus
'Archer's Gold'
- Evergreen perennial,
  herb
- To 12"
- Summer
- Pale lavender
- Zones 6–9

- Sun
- Source: fff
A creeping thyme used
mostly for ornamental
purposes. Leaves have
gold edge. Good for a
rock garden or to edge
a path.

tricolor sage

Salvia officinalis 'Tricolor'
- Perennial, shrub
- 18"
- Summer
- Foliage plant—pink, green, and cream leaves
- Aromatic foliage
- Zones 7–9
- Sun, light shade
- Sources: n, oo, fff

Doesn't do well in hot, humid climates; treat as an annual in those areas. Dies in heavy clay; must have very good drainage.

lemon balm

Melissa officinalis
- Perennial, herb
- 24"
- Late summer
- Fragrant
- Yellow-white
- Zones 4–7
- Sun, partial shade
- Sources: n, vv, fff

Easy to grow; will reseed. Light green leaves with lemon scent; dries well. Use fresh in green or fruit salads, with fish dishes, and in drinks.

golden sage

Salvia officinalis 'Icterina'
- Perennial, shrub
- 12–24"
- Foliage plant—yellow and green leaves
- Aromatic
- Zones 5–8
- Sun, light shade
- Sources: n, fff

Ornamental and culinary sage with variegated green and gold leaves. Attractive mixed with yellow flowers and darker greens.

purple basil

Ocimum basilicum 'Dark Opal'
- Annual, herb
- 24"
- Summer, early fall
- Pink
- Aromatic foliage
- Sun
- Sources: m, kk, xx.

Deep reddish purple leaves are stunning in the garden. Use in the kitchen as you would sweet basil—imparts a lovely color to vinegar.

globe amaranth

Gomphrena globosa
- Annual
- 12–24″
- Summer to fall
- Pink, purple, red, white
- Sun
- Sources: uu, bbb

Not an edible amaranth but very nice in the garden. Good cut flower. Hang cut bunches upside down to dry for winter arrangements.

borage

Borago officinalis
- Annual, herb
- To 3′
- Spring through fall
- Blue
- Sun
- Sources: ii, oo, fff

Easy to grow in most soils, if well-drained. Reseeds readily. Hairy leaves are edible, with cucumber flavor but a rather strange texture. To enjoy the edible flowers, remove the stamens first.

rosemary

Rosmarinus officinalis
'Miss Jessopp's Upright'
- Shrub, evergreen
- 4–5′
- Winter, spring
- Fragrant
- Light blue
- Zones 6–10
- Sun, partial sun
- Sources: n, fff

Strong upright growth. Can be pruned and trained as a topiary standard. Needs good drainage.

tall marigold

Tagetes erecta hyb.
- Annual
- 1–4′
- Summer to frost
- Orange and yellow
- Sun
- Sources: u, w, ii, kk, ss, aaa

Stately plants with vivid colors; much more dramatic than the compact dwarfs. Some may require staking but are certainly worth it. Good as cut flowers, but change water daily. Flowers are not edible.

sage

Salvia officinalis
- Evergreen perennial, herb
- 2–3′
- Summer
- Lilac blue
- Aromatic gray-green leaves
- Zones 3–10
- Sun
- Sources: d, m, n, u, oo, uu, fff

Must have well-drained soil; not good in humid heat of the South. Protect with mulch in coldest areas. Favored for stuffing, sausage, and poultry.

cinnamon basil

Ocimum basilicum
'Cinnamon'
- Annual, herb
- 2½′
- Summer, early fall
- Aromatic foliage
- Lavender with white
- Sun
- Sources: e, h, ff, oo

The delicately-scented leaves have a matte finish and purple stems. Leaves and flowers are edible; or add them to bouquets of flowers.

garlic chives

Allium tuberosum
- Perennial, bulb
- 18–30″
- Summer
- White
- Zones 4–8
- Sun
- Sources: ii, kk, vv, zz, aaa

The leaves and edible flowers have a strong garlic flavor. They look great growing among other herbs and flowers. Reseeds readily; deadhead to avoid too many plants.

dwarf marigold

Tagetes hyb.
- Annual
- 6–18″
- Summer to frost
- Yellow, orange, maroon
- Sun
- Sources: e, ii, zz, bbb

Easy-to-grow plants; start seeds in warm soil. Deadhead blooms to keep flowers coming. Good for the edge of a border or in containers.

golden oregano

Origanum vulgare
'Aureum'
- Perennial
- 12"
- Spring–mid-summer
- Lavender-pink
- Zones 5–9
- Sun
- Sources: oo, fff

Good in rock gardens. Also called golden marjoram. Mild oregano flavor.

cilantro/coriander

Coriandrum sativum
- Annual, herb
- 12–15"
- Summer to fall
- White to pale purple

- Sun, partial shade
- Source: uu

Called cilantro when grown for its fern-like leaves; coriander when grown for seed. Flower stalks can grow to 3'. Succession sow if growing for leaves. Day-length sensitive; will go to seed quickly if planted before July.

italian oregano

Origanum vulgare
- Perennial, herb
- 12–36"
- Spring to early fall
- Aromatic foliage
- Pink or white
- Zones 5–9
- Sun
- Source: oo

Prefers poor to medium, well-drained soil. Cut back in spring. Enhances many dishes; often used with tomato sauces; combines well with garlic and thyme.

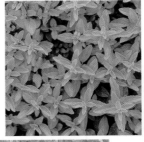

chervil

Anthriscus cerefolium
- Annual, herb
- 24"
- Summer
- White
- Sun, partial shade
- Source: h

Lacy leaves have a slightly anise flavor. One of the French fines herbes, it has many culinary uses. Grows best in cool weather.

grain amaranth

Amaranthus cruentus
(*A. paniculatus*)
- Annual
- To 6'
- Summer to fall
- Red-green
- Sun
- Sources: w, dd, ss

Long cymes of flowers are followed by red, purple, or yellow seed heads. Seed is a very nutritious grain. After harvesting, lay on a tarp for a week until dry, then thresh.

french sorrel

Rumex scutatus
- Perennial, herb
- 6"
- Summer
- Green with pink, red, rust
- Zones 3–10
- Sun
- Sources: n, fff

The true French sorrel, grown for its slightly lemon-flavored leaves. Does well in all but the harshest of climates.

summer savory

Satureja hortensis
- Annual, herb
- 10"
- Summer
- Pink
- Sun
- Sources: ii, oo, fff

Keep well-watered. Does well in containers. Start harvesting when 6" tall. Spicy flavor—use with eggs, pasta, meat, beans, other vegetables, and in soups.

woolly thyme

Thymus pseudolanuginosis
- Perennial
- 2–3"
- Midsummer
- Pale pink, lavender-pink
- Zones 5–9
- Sun
- Sources: n, oo, fff

Creeping thyme with small, woolly leaves. 'Hall's Woody' is the fastest-growing; not as woolly and blooms more than the species.

lemon-scented geranium

Pelargonium crispum
- Perennial, subshrub
- 3'
- Spring, summer
- Pink
- Aromatic foliage
- Zone 10
- Sun
- Sources: n, z, oo

Small, crinkled leaves with strong lemon scent. There are other lemon-scented hybrids.

cottage pinks

Dianthus plumarius hyb.
- Perennial
- 12–16"
- Spring to fall
- Fragrant
- White to red
- Zones 3–10
- Sun, light afternoon shade
- Sources: f, u, ii, zz, iii

Single or double, edible flowers—some with a spicy, clove fragrance. Nice in small bouquets. Doesn't like the humid heat of the Deep South.

lemon thyme

Thymus × citriodorus
- Evergreen perennial, herb
- To 12"
- Summer
- Pale lilac
- Zones 6–9
- Sun
- Sources: e, n, oo, fff

Upright or spreading. Smells wonderful just to brush against. Edible flowers and leaves go nicely with poultry. The leaves can be dried or preserved in vinegar or oil.

front-
yard
garden

Kitchen gardens don't have to be hidden beside the back door, as this front-yard in Bainbridge Island, Washington, proves. A formal herb garden with a Gallic flair, it was inspired by the symmetry of gardens found in French chàteau country. Here, a kitchen garden filled with herbs and flowers grows as full and rich as many flower gardens and in full view of passersby. Fragrant, useful, and beautiful plants meld into a front-yard of refined whimsy.

a

fter Sarah Pearl and Barry Sacks purchased their first home on Bainbridge Island, they based their front-yard garden on a geometrical layout,

creating a dooryard entry

low boxwood hedge repeats the shape while doubling as an evergreen background for flowers such as 'Lemon Gem' marigolds and Johnny-jump-ups. The year-round greenery is important to Sarah, who tends the garden well past the growing season to keep the

echoing the symmetrical designs of gardens they had visited in France. As an expert cook, Barry naturally wanted to grow herbs in the new garden. Including annuals, roses, and fruit trees in the plant palette added highlights to the composition.

The garden's central bed is diamond-shaped—a popular French motif. Wheelbarrow-wide pathways of crushed stone are contained by treated cherry ties. The angular paths shape perimeter planting beds and emphasize the diamond design. A

front-yard appealing.

After trial and error taught Sarah to avoid crowding too many 4-inch plants together, she successfully filled the center bed with a cream, gray, and yellow combination of santolina, lavender, feverfew, and yellow roses. A clematis winds its way with tantalizing grace through the rings of an armillary sphere, which adds formal grace to the garden.

Elsewhere in the garden, a wealth of herbs thrives in double-dug beds. Like other gardeners, Sarah and Barry cherish the special pass-along plants that have been given to them. Sages, chamomile, and thyme were gifts from Sarah's sister's garden. Barry harvests dill for pickling and for adding exotic flavors to his cooking experiments.

Research and experience led Sarah and Barry to realize that

grouping similar herbs helps minimize maintenance. For example, drought-tolerant Mediterranean herbs—rosemary, thyme, curry, marjoram, oregano, and chives—grow well together in a bed, rarely requiring any extra water.

The front-yard has proven to be the right spot for Sarah and Barry's efforts. As pretty as it is practical, the garden acts as a living welcome mat to their home, while contributing fresh flavors to the kitchen.

GARDEN ORNAMENTS

There are a few ornaments that always are aesthetically correct in an herb or kitchen garden. Sundials and armillary spheres have a long history of practical and ornamental use.

Sundials measure time by casting a shadow on a flat surface marked with the times of day. Armillary spheres depict the heavens encircling the earth. The arrow that is pointed toward the North Pole casts a shadow on the equatorial ring and will also give you a reading of local sun time.

The most durable sundials and armillary spheres are constructed of metal. Either can be an effective focal point for an herb garden. Place one on a plain base, as simple as a section of log or, for a more formal look, a short stone column.

A strawberry pot is perfect for growing herbs or succulents, as shown here. *Opposite:* Overview of the garden.

It takes courage to **dig up** a front-yard, even for veteran gardeners. For Sarah Pearl and Barry Sacks, whose previous gardening experience was limited to growing potted plants on an apartment deck, the task could have been daunting. Instead, they focused on their shared vision— their memories of the formal gardens of French chateàux. They transplanted that geometric formality to their own acre-and-a-half property, with great results. Sarah and Barry love dining outside, especially during the summer, when daylight pleasantly lingers well past dinnertime.

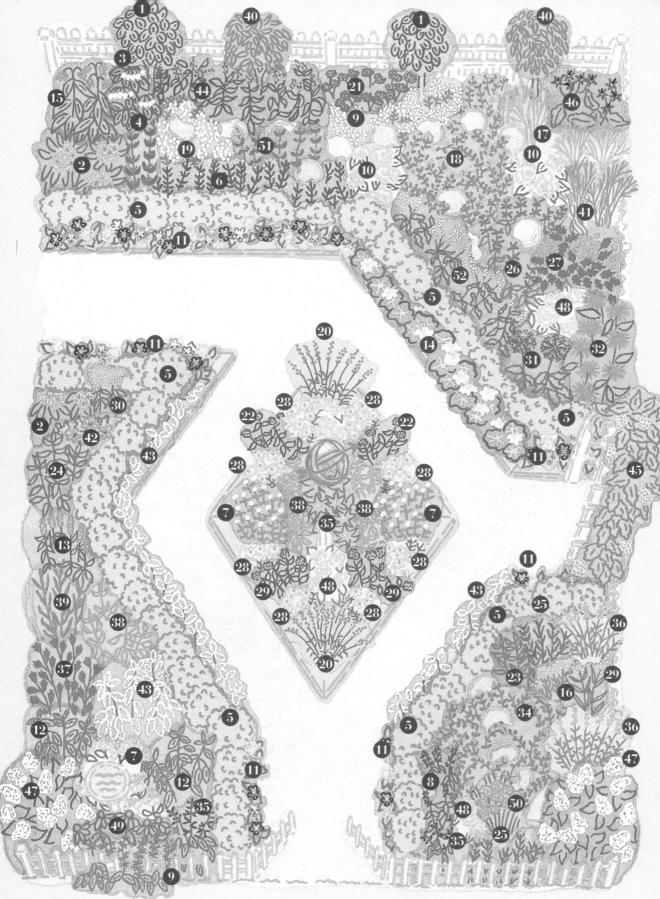

1. Dwarf Pear
2. Winter Daphne
3. Wintergreen
4. Hyssop
5. Dwarf Boxwood
6. Winter Savory
7. Evening Primrose
8. Catmint
9. Clary Sage
10. Shrub Rose
11. Pansy
12. Sage
13. Anise Hyssop
14. Nasturtium
15. Comfrey
16. Curry Plant
17. Bronze Fennel
18. Lemon Thyme
19. Golden Feverfew
20. French Lavender
21. Curly Parsley
22. Heliotrope
23. Spearmint
24. Peppermint
25. Pink-Flowered Rosemary
26. Siberian Catmint
27. Germander
28. Signet Marigold
29. Weld
30. Lemon Verbena

dwarf pear

Pyrus spp.
- Deciduous fruit tree
- To 15′
- Spring flowers
- White
- Zones 4–9
- Sun
- Source: mm

Dwarf pear trees are ideal for gardeners with small lots. They can be used for hedges or grown in containers.

winter daphne

Daphne odora
- Evergreen shrub
- To 6′
- Winter–spring
- Fragrant
- Pale pink, purplish red in bud
- Zones 7–9
- Sun, partial shade
- Source: l

Sweetly fragrant flowers. Prefers well-drained soil; doesn't like to dry out. Keep the roots moist in summer with mulch.

wintergreen

Gaultheria procumbens
- Evergreen shrublet
- 6″, spreads to 3′
- Summer
- Pinkish white
- Zones 3–8
- Partial shade
- Source: eee

Urn-shaped flowers followed by scarlet berries. Fruit and leaves have wintergreen taste. Use as ground cover in woodland plantings. Prefers acid soil.

hyssop

Hyssopus officinalis
- Evergreen, herb
- 1–2′
- Summer to fall
- Blue, pink
- Aromatic foliage
- Zones 6–9
- Sun, partial shade
- Sources: h, oo, aaa, fff

Attractive as a low-growing hedge; use in knot gardens or as a border. Edible flowers and leaves have a bitter, tonic-like flavor.

dwarf boxwood

Buxus microphylla hyb.
- Evergreen shrub
- 1–3′
- Foliage plant
- Zones 4–9, varies by cultivars
- Sun or shade
- Source: l

Compact plants with dark green leaves. Perfect for low hedges.

winter savory

Satureja montana
- Perennial, herb
- 16″
- Summer, fall
- White to pale violet
- Zones 5–8

- Sun
- Source: w

Semi-evergreen. Edible flowers and leaves have a rather heavy aroma and stronger taste than summer savory. Often used as a seasoning with game meats.

evening primrose

Oenothera elata ssp. *hookeri* (*O. hookeri*)
- Perennial
- 3'
- Summer
- Pale yellow to orange-red
- Zones 7–9
- Sun
- Source: ss

Flowers open at dusk. Native to western America. Grows in poor soil, well-drained soil.

clary sage

Salvia sclarea
- Biennial
- 3–5'
- Spring, summer
- White, pink, blue
- Zones 5–9
- Sun
- Sources: n, tt, fff

Popular herb with large leaves; spikes of 1-inch flowers the second year. Leaves have a rather medicinal smell. Self-sows readily in the garden.

catmint

Nepeta × *faassenii*
- Perennial
- 2'–3'
- Spring through fall
- Blue
- Zones 4–9
- Sun
- Source: jjj

Low-maintenance plant. Trim back and tidy it up after flowering to encourage more blooming. May not tolerate the heat and high humidity of the Deep South.

shrub rose

Rosa Graham Thomas ™
- Shrub
- 5–7'
- Spring to fall
- Fragrant
- Yellow
- Zones 5–9
- Sun
- Source: jjj

A David Austin English rose with bright green leaves and an arching habit. Big, old-fashioned double blossoms. Flowers edible if not sprayed.

pansy

Viola x *wittrockiana*
- Annual
- 6–9"
- Spring, early summer
- White to purple
- Sun, partial shade
- Sources: ii, zz, bbb

Pansies give welcome color early in the season and in winter in mild climates. They like rich, moist soil and afternoon shade in hot areas. Edible flowers are a lovely garnish on pasta or canapes.

anise hyssop

Agastache foeniculum
- Perennial
- 3–5'
- Summer
- Aromatic leaves
- Lavender-purple
- Zones 6–10
- Sun
- Sources: h, vv, fff

Sweet, licorice-flavored edible flowers. Use young leaves and flower petals in salads, drinks, soups, and mushrooms dishes.

sage

Salvia officinalis
- Perennial, herb
- 2–3'
- Summer
- Lilac blue
- Aromatic gray-green leaves
- Zones 3–10
- Sun
- Sources: d, m, n, u, oo, uu, fff

Pungent herb; start from cuttings or seeds. Does poorly in hot, humid climates or heavy clay. Give winter protection in coldest regions.

nasturtium

Tropaeolum majus
'Whirlybird'
- Annual
- 12"
- Spring to fall
- Mixed colors
- Sun, partial shade
- Sources: ii, uu, zz, bbb

Upward-facing blossoms. Edible flowers and leaves have a peppery flavor. Early blooming, vigorous plants. Good for hanging baskets. Self-sows in mild climates.

comfrey

Symphytum officinale
- Perennial, herb
- 3–5'
- Spring to frost
- White to red
- Zones 3–10
- Sun, partial shade
- Sources: n, oo, fff

Ornamental only—not for culinary or medicinal use. Easy, fast-growing, background plant. Can be invasive.

curry plant

Helichrysum italicum (H. angustifolium)
- Shrub
- 16"
- Summer to fall
- Yellow
- Zones 7–10
- Sun
- Sources: oo, fff

Ornamental landscape plant. Silver-gray leaves have a curry fragrance; they are not edible (curry is a blend of spices). Needs well-drained soil, neutral to alkaline pH.

bronze fennel

Foeniculum vulgare 'Smokey'
- Perennial, herb
- 4–5'
- Summer, fall
- Yellow

- Zones 4–10
- Sun
- Sources: h, uu, oo, aaa

The ferny leaves of this fennel are bronzered. Grow for its ornamental qualities, as an herb, or to attract beneficial insects. Reseeds easily.

lemon thyme

Thymus × citriodorus
- Evergreen perennial, herb
- To 12"
- Summer
- Pale lilac
- Zones 6–9
- Sun
- Sources: e, n, oo, fff

Plant where you can enjoy the fragrant foliage. Perfect in a rock garden, along a path, at the edge of beds, or mixed with other thymes.

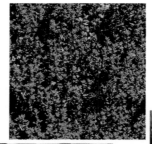

golden feverfew

Tanacetum parthenium (Chrysanthemum parthenium) hyb.
- Perennial
- 18–24"
- Summer
- Yellow-tinted white
- Zones 4–9
- Sun
- Sources: tt, uu, zz

A bushy, branching plant usually covered with many small daisy-like flowers. Prefers well-drained soil. Self sows.

german chamomile

Matricaria recutita
- Annual, herb
- 6"–24"
- Summer
- Fragrant
- White with yellow center
- Sun, partial shade

- Sources: w, ff, tt, uu

Used for cooking more than perennial chamomile. Best to sow seeds in the fall; freezing and thawing helps germination. Dry flowers for tea.

french lavender

Lavandula dentata
- Shrub
- To 3'
- Spring, summer
- Fragrant
- Light lavender
- Sun
- Zones 8–10
- Sources: n, oo, fff, iii

Does not do well in the humid heat of the South. Blooms nonstop along the Pacific Coast. Narrow leaves have small indentations on margins. Needs well-drained soil.

curly parsley

Petroselinum crispum
- Biennial grown as annual
- 10–18"
- Flowers 2nd year
- White
- Sun, partial shade
- Sources: q, w, ff, ii

Pretty in the garden. Use as a border, or mix with pansies or other low-growing annual flowers. Nutritious, use in the kitchen for its flavor, not just as a garnish.

heliotrope

Heliotropum arborescens
- Perennial grown as annual
- 18″ in containers, 3–4′ in ground
- Fragrant
- Violet, purple to white
- Zones 10–11
- Sources: tt, zz, bbb

Flowers have a lovely vanilla fragrance—especially fragrant at night. Dark green leaves are often tinged with purple. Use in containers or mixed border.

peppermint

Mentha × piperita
- Perennial
- 12–36″, spreading
- Summer
- Lilac-pink
- Aromatic foliage
- Zones 3–7
- Sun, partial shade
- Sources: n, oo, fff

A bit strong for most culinary uses. Thrives in drier, milder regions of zones 8–10. Invasive; plant in containers or sink a barrier at least 10″

spearmint

Mentha spicata
- Perennial
- To 3′, spreading
- Summer
- Pink, white, lilac
- Aromatic foliage
- Zones 3–7
- Sun, partial shade
- Sources: tt, zz, bbb

The bright green leaves are smaller and milder-tasting than peppermint. Delightful in cold drinks; great with lamb. Edible flowers. Invasive.

pink-flowered rosemary

Rosmarinus officinalis hyb.
- Evergreen shrub
- 2–4′
- Winter, spring in West
- Fragrant
- Pink
- Zones 8–10
- Sun, partial sun
- Source: fff

'Majorca Pink', 'Pinkie', and 'Roseus' are pink-flowered. Needs well-drained soil.

germander

Teucrium gussonei
(*T. cossonii*) hyb.
- Perennial
- 8″ tall, 18″ wide
- Summer
- Vivid violet-purple
- Zones 7–9
- Sun
- Source: ww

Gray foliage with sweet lavender scent. Likes lean soil with grit in it. Fairly drought-tolerant.

lemon verbena

Aloysia triphylla
- Shrub, tender
- 3–6′
- Summer
- Fragrant
- Pale pink
- Zones 8–11
- Sun, part shade
- Sources: z, ff, oo

Prune often to keep trim and bushy. Use leaves to flavor fish, tea, chicken, fruit drinks.

siberian catmint

Nepeta sibirica
- Perennial
- 2′–3′
- Spring through fall
- Purplish blue

- Zones 3–8
- Sun
- Sources: iii, jjj

Ornamental landscape plant with mildly aromatic foliage. Easy to grow, requires only minimum maintenance.

weld

Reseda luteola
- Annual or perennial
- To 4½′
- Late summer to fall
- Yellowish green
- Sun
- Source: oo

Used for centuries as a source of yellow dye for wool, cotton, or silk. Likes well-drained soil. Blooms earlier on the Pacific Coast. Might reseed.

bee balm

Monarda didyma
'Mahogany'
- Perennial
- 3′
- Summer

- Aromatic foliage
- Deep wine red
- Zones 4–9
- Sun
- Sources: c, n, eee

Has shown some powdery mildew resistance. Not only bees but hummingbirds like monarda, too.

signet marigold

Tagetes tenuifolia
'Lemon Gem'
- Annual
- 8″
- Summer
- Yellow
- Sun
- Sources: h, w, uu

Mounds of lacy foliage covered with small, edible flowers. Flowers have a citrusy tarragon flavor.

giant angelica

Angelica gigas
- Biennial
- 3–6′
- Late summer, early fall
- Dark purple
- Zones 4–9
- Sun, partial shade, shade
- Sources: ggg, jjj

Large dramatic plant with tall, red flower stems topped by purple umbels. Likes moist loam. Bees love it.

clematis

Clematis 'Comtesse de Bouchaud'
- Perennial, vine
- 6–10'
- Summer into fall
- Mauve pink
- Zones 4–9
- Sun, partial shade
- Source: jjj

Abundant, large flowers. Mulch and/or grow where other plants will shade the root area.

thyme

Thymus vulgaris
- Evergreen perennial, herb
- 6–12″
- Late spring, summer
- Aromatic foliage
- Lilac

- Zones 4–9
- Sun
- Sources: n, oo, fff

Cut thyme back in spring by one-third to keep it lush. In cold regions, protect with a winter mulch. Thyme is quite pest- and disease-resistant.

pineapple sage

Salvia elegans
- Perennial, herb
- 6′
- Late summer, fall, winter
- Bright red
- Zones 8–10
- Sun
- Sources: e, n, oo, fff

Bright, tasty edible flowers and scented foliage. Fast-growing. Likes well-drained soil.

english lavender

Lavandula angustifolia 'Munstead'
- Shrub
- 12–18″
- Summer
- Fragrant
- Lavender
- Sun
- Zones 5–10
- Sources: s, eee, fff, jjj,

Lavenders do beautifully in the drier, milder-climate areas of zones 8–10, but don't like the continuous heat and humidity of the Deep South.

lovage

Levisticum officinale
- Perennial, herb
- 2–6′
- Summer
- Greenish yellow
- Zones 3–9
- Sun, partial shade
- Sources: e, u, w, ii, vv

Grows very large in moist areas; give plenty of room. Reseeds readily; keep seed heads cut off unless you want to harvest them.

golden oregano

Origanum vulgare 'Aureum'
- Perennial, herb
- 12″
- Spring to midsummer
- Aromatic leaves
- Lavender-pink
- Zones 5–9
- Sun
- Sources: oo, fff

Very ornamental with its aromatic golden leaves. Needs well-drained soil. Also known as golden marjoram.

french tarragon

Artemisia dracunculus
- Perennial, herb
- 2–3′
- Summer
- Greenish white flowers
- Aromatic foliage
- Zones 4–10
- Sun, partial shade
- Sources: h, n, ii, oo, fff

Not for the humid South. Harvest anytime during growing season. Use sparingly in sauces.

plum

Prunus americana × simonii 'Toka'
- Deciduous fruit tree
- To 15′
- Spring
- White
- Zones 3–7

- Sun
- Source: yy

Hardy northern plum, to -50° F. Bears late August through September. Fruit is reddish bronze with a blue blush and has a wonderful, rich, spicy-sweet, yellow flesh.

florence fennel

Foeniculum vulgare var. *azoricum* 'Fino'
- Biennial
- 12"
- Flowers 2nd year
- Yellow
- Zones 4–10
- Sun
- Sources: h, w, ii, uu, oo, aaa

Grown for its swollen, bulb-like leaf bases, which have a mild anise flavor and crisp texture.

golden sage

Salvia officinalis 'Icterina'
- Perennial, shrub
- 12–24"
- Foliage plant—green and yellow leaves
- Aromatic
- Zones 5–8
- Sun, light shade
- Sources: n, fff

Gold variegated leaves. Less vigorous variety of culinary sage. Prefers well-drained soil. Cut back in spring. Use leaves as you would culinary sage.

scented geranium

Pelargonium 'Gray Lady Plymouth'
- Perennial, subshrub
- 1–3'
- Spring, summer
- Aromatic foliage
- Pink
- Zones 9–10
- Sun
- Sources: n, oo, fff

Gray-green leaves with fine, white edge; rose-scented.

basil

Ocimum basilicum 'Siam Queen'
- Annual, herb
- To 30"
- Summer, fall
- Aromatic foliage
- Burgundy
- Sun
- Sources: w, ii

The bright green leaves have an intense anise-basil flavor that is perfect for Southeast Asian cuisine. Ornamental and high-yielding plant.

hops

Humulus lupulus
- Perennial, vine
- 15–20'
- Summer
- Papery green flowers
- Zones 4–10
- Sun
- Sources: n, oo

Fast-growing vine that makes a quick screen. Needs a trellis or other support. Flowers and tender young shoots are edible.

lilac

Syringa vulgaris
- Shrub
- To 20'
- Spring
- Fragrant
- Pink, white, lavender
- Zones 4–8
- Sun
- Sources: ggg, local nurseries

Loved for fabulous fragrance and voluptuous blossoms. Nondescript shrubs rest of the year. Prone to powdery mildew. Needs winter chill to bloom.

borage

Borago officinalis
- Annual, herb
- To 3'
- Spring through fall
- Aromatic foliage
- Blue
- Sun
- Sources: h, ii, oo, fff

Reseeds readily, but it's fun to let it come up serendipitously (and it's easy to weed out unwanted seedlings). Flowers and young leaves have cucumber flavor.

floribunda rose

Rosa 'Sun Flare'
- Shrub
- 2–3'
- Summer
- Fragrant
- Bright yellow
- Zones 5–9
- Sun
- Source: v

Has an unusual, mild licorice scent. Cold-tolerant and disease-resistant. Edible flowers.

purple coneflower

Echinacea purpurea
- Perennial
- 2–4′
- Summer to fall
- Purplish pink
- Zones 3–10
- Sun
- Sources: ee, ll, bbb

Easy-to-grow North American native. Handsome 3-inch daisy-like flowers. Likes well-drained soil.

pennyroyal

Mentha pulegium
- Perennial, herb
- 4–16″
- Summer
- Aromatic foliage
- Lilac
- Zones 7–9
- Sun
- Sources: n, oo, fff

Ornamental; not to be taken internally. Used as a natural insect repellent. Use in herb and rock gardens, along bed edges.

chives

Allium schoenoprasum
- Perennial, bulb
- 12–18″
- Early summer
- Lavender
- Zones 3–9
- Sun
- Sources: ii, kk, oo, vv, zz, aaa

Chives are easy to grow and easy to cook with. Edible flowers and leaves can be used as an onion substitute. Prefers a moist, moderately fertile soil.

holy basil

Ocimum tenuiflorum
(*O. sanctum*)
- Annual, herb
- To 3′
- Summer
- Aromatic foliage
- Pink or white
- Sun
- Sources: w, uu

Ornamental; not usually used in cooking. Sweetly aromatic foliage. Long revered by the Hindus of India.

cottage

style

h

erbs, flowers, and vegetables mingle in this New Jersey yard, where cottage-style gardening translates into joyful abundance. Clematis clambers up a fence, roses ramble, and thyme fills the crevices of fieldstone paths. The seeming disarray belies its careful planning. The old barn's foundation provides the framework and controls the exuberance of the herb garden. Raised beds make it practical.

Plant an old basket with herbs and flowers—it's readily moved to grace any area. *Opposite*: Golden feverfew.

england's original cottage gardens were little more than kitchen gardens run delightfully amok. Cultivated by cottage dwellers who toiled on large estates, these small patches of land yielded food, seasonings, medicines, and dyes. With so much growing in so little space, gardens overflowed with abundance. Flowers and foliage spilled across pathways, roses and vining vegetables tumbled over tidy fences, and herbs grew everywhere.

For years, Clarabel Kent dreamed of a cottage-style garden of her own and collected books on the subject. Then her husband Jim built a large stone cottage complete with gables and a sloping roofline, nestled on two acres of land in Long Valley, New Jersey. Clarabel's ideas finally took root. In a 20×20-foot plot rimmed by the stone foundation left from an old barn, a garden now grows. Brick pathways, laid without mortar, give the garden shape, while wooden edging forms raised beds. Elevating the planting areas gave Clarabel the opportunity to add soil rich in organic matter; it also improved drainage, an important factor when cultivating herbs.

The slight change in soil height has aesthetic value as well. Rather than staying in a flat plane, plants grow up and over, weaving a tapestry of color and texture. Poppies, foxgloves, and roses add their colorful blossoms to the composition, while sweet woodruff, sage, lamb's-ears, thyme, and many others contribute shades of green and silver.

A limited color palette keeps the profusion from becoming overwhelming. Cool pastels—pinks, blues, and purples—dominate the scheme. The repetition of hues throughout the beds is lovely. It also helps a garden of variety grow as a harmonious composition.

Other plants are grown for fragrance and flavor. Rosemary and thyme top Clarabel's list of cooking favorites, but she also grows many selections of scented geraniums in the garden, including apricot, nutmeg, peppermint, lemon, and rose.

creating a cottage-style garden

SWEET BAY

Sweet bay goes by many names—bay tree, laurel, and bay laurel. It figures in Greek mythology as a laurel. Apollo was smitten with the fair nymph Daphne, but she wanted to have nothing to do with him. While Apollo pursued her, she cried out for help, and her father turned her into a sweet bay. Apollo then fell on his knees in front of the tree and declared it eternally sacred. He then made a wreath of laurel leaves, which he wore on his head from that day forward.

The tree remained a symbol of glory and reward. Laurel garlands were presented to the champions at the first Olympics. The herb has been prescribed as a medicinal herb since the Middle Ages.

Today, sweet bay is often trained into standard topiary. The leaves, which make lovely wreaths, are used in stews and ragouts.

Birds come to use the birdbath and help keep insects at bay. *Opposite:* Overview of the garden.

Passionate about English-style gardening, Clarabel and Jim Kent transformed their New Jersey home and garden to resemble the ones in the English countryside. Jim built their house, although its gables, sloping roofline, and stone facade look as if they were transported from one of the lovely homes of England. Once the house was complete, Clarabel set about putting into practice the knowledge garnered from years of studying about herbs and cottage gardens. Today, a bit of English tradition lives on in America, as the Kents harvest from the graceful tangle of colorful and culinary plantings.

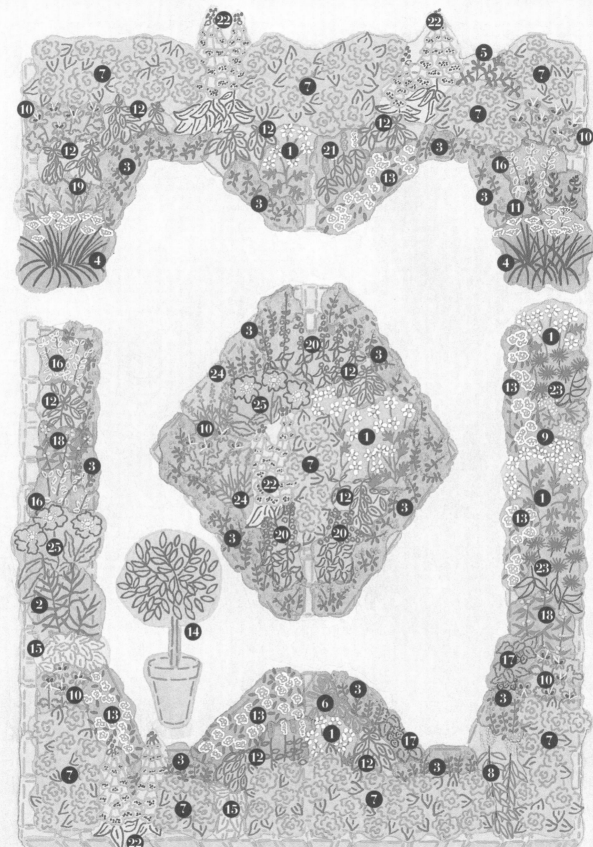

1. Golden Feverfew
2. French Tarragon
3. Caraway Thyme
4. Garlic Chives
5. Rue
6. Lamb's-Ears
7. Shrub Rose
8. Lemon Verbena
9. Lady's-Mantle
10. Scented Geranium
11. Anise Hyssop
12. Sage
13. Sweet Alyssum
14. Sweet Bay
15. Golden Lemon Balm
16. Sweet Marjoram
17. Alpine Strawberry
18. Summer Savory
19. Rosemary
20. Catmint
21. Hyssop
22. Foxglove
23. Bee Balm
24. Lavender
25. Breadseed Poppy

golden feverfew

Tanacetum parthenium
(Chrysanthemum
parthenium) hyb.
- Perennial
- 18–24"
- Summer
- Yellow-tinted white
- Zones 4–9
- Sun
- Sources: tt, uu, zz

A bushy, branching plant, often covered with many small, daisy-like flowers. Prefers well-drained soil. Self sows.

french tarragon

Artemisia dracunculus
- Perennial, herb
- 2–3'
- Aromatic foliage
- Dark blue-green leaves
- Full sun, part shade
- Zones 4–10
- Sources: h, n, oo, fff

Does not do well in humid heat of the South. Needs well-drained soil. Use in sauces, salad dressings, with fish and meats to add an anise flavor.

caraway thyme

Thymus herba-barona
- Evergreen perennial, herb
- To 4"
- Midsummer
- Aromatic foliage

- Rose pink
- Zones 6–9
- Sun
- Sources: n, oo, fff

Ornamental and culinary. Leaves have caraway scent and flavor. Edible flowers. Quick-growing; spreads to form a mat of tiny leaves.

garlic chives

Allium tuberosum
- Perennial, bulb
- 18–30"
- Summer
- White
- Zones 4–8
- Sun
- Sources: ii, kk, vv, zz, aaa

Also called Oriental chives. Clusters of star-shaped, edible flowers. Plant in spring from divisions, transplants, or seeds. Self sows.

rue

Ruta graveolens
- Perennial
- 2–3'
- Summer
- Yellow
- Zones 5–9
- Sun
- Sources: n, oo, fff

Take care when growing rue, as the leaves may cause allergic skin reactions. A silvery plant to place between hot-colored flowers in the garden.

lamb's-ears

Stachys byzantina hyb.
- Perennial
- 3'
- Summer
- White and purple, pink
- Zones 4–9
- Sun
- Sources: c, s, iii

Soft, woolly leaves and erect stems of flowers. Leaf colors of cultivars range from silver-gray to medium green, brushed with silver.

shrub rose

Rosa Carefree Beauty™
- Shrub
- 5'
- Spring to fall
- Fragrant
- Light pink
- Zones 4–9
- Sun
- Source: g

Clusters of semidouble blossoms and olive green leaves. Rose petals are edible if never sprayed with pesticide.

lemon verbena

Aloysia triphylla
- Shrub, tender
- 3–6'
- Summer
- Fragrant
- Pale pink
- Zones 8–11
- Sun, part shade
- Sources: z, ff, oo

Needs well-drained soil. Has a gangly habit. Young leaves at the top of the plant are best for culinary use.

lady's mantle

Alchemilla mollis
- Perennial
- 3'
- Summer
- Yellow
- Zones 3–7
- Sun, partial shade
- Sources: f, eee, jjj

After chartreuse flowers fade, deadhead either by cutting the flower stems or pulling them out at the base. May reseed.

anise hyssop

Agastache foeniculum hyb.
- Perennial
- 3–5'
- Summer
- Aromatic foliage
- Blue
- Zones 6–10
- Sun
- Sources: h, vv, fff

Easy to grow. Leaves and flowers have a sweet, anise scent, and both are edible. Flowers are used in baking and sauteing mushrooms.

scented geranium

Pelargonium hyb.
- Perennial, subshrub
- 1–4'
- Spring, summer
- Aromatic foliage
- White to purple
- Zones 9–10
- Sun
- Sources: gn, z, oo, fff

Grown for the aromatic foliage. Clusters of small, single, edible flowers.

sage

Salvia officinalis 'Berggarten'
- Perennial, herb
- 24"
- Summer
- Aromatic foliage
- Nonflowering
- Zones 4–9
- Sun, light shade
- Sources: oo, fff

A vigorous plant with large gray leaves. If sages get leggy, cut them back in the spring and again in summer.

sweet alyssum

Lobularia maritima
- Annual
- 2–12″
- Spring to frost
- White
- Sun
- Sources: ii, uu, zz, bbb

Easy to grow. Likes light, well-drained soil. Blooms all year in mild-winter regions. Will reseed.

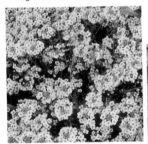

sweet bay

Laurus nobilis
- Evergreen shrub or tree
- 12–40′
- Spring
- Aromatic foliage
- Greenish yellow
- Zones 8–10
- Sun, partial shade
- Sources: n, hh

Bay leaves are used in cooking. Tolerates pruning and is sometimes used as topiary. Contact with the foliage may cause skin allergies.

golden lemon balm

Melissa officinalis 'Aurea'
- Perennial, herb
- 24″
- Late summer

- Fragrant
- Yellow-white
- Zones 4–7
- Sun, partial shade
- Sources: n, vv, fff

Keep the seed heads cut off or it will reseed and may become a nuisance. Has citrus flavor. Use as you would mint leaves.

sweet marjoram

Origanum marjorana
- Perennial, herb
- 12″
- Late summer, fall
- Aromatic foliage
- White or pink
- Zones 8–10
- Sun
- Sources: h, w, ii, oo, fff

Also called knotted marjoram—flower buds look like little knots. Use the edible flowers and leaves in cooking.

alpine strawberry

Fragaria vesca 'Semperflorens' (*F. alpina semperflorens*)
- Perennial, fruit
- 6–12″
- Spring, summer
- White
- Zones 5–10
- Sun, light shade
- Sources: w, uu

Small, intensely flavored red berries. Good plants for containers, hanging baskets, or a groundcover in small spaces.

summer savory

Satureja hortensis
- Annual, herb
- 10″
- Summer
- Pink
- Sun
- Sources: ii, oo, fff

Easy to grow; blooms all summer long. Edible flowers. Nice in a flower border or an herb garden. Grows well in a container.

rosemary

Rosmarinus officinalis 'Golden Rain'
- Shrub, evergreen
- 2′
- Winter, spring
- Fragrant
- Dark violet-blue
- Zones 7–10
- Sun, partial sun
- Sources: n, oo, fff

Unusual cultivar with green and gold variegation, which tends to fade in summer.

catmint

Nepeta × *faassenii* hyb.
- Perennial
- 2–3′
- Spring through fall
- Blue
- Zones 4–9
- Sun
- Source: jjj

Lovely in a raised bed, draping softly over the side. Durable, heavy-flowering plants; pestfree.

hyssop

Hyssopus officinalis
- Evergreen, herb
- 1–2′
- Summer to fall
- Blue, pink
- Aromatic foliage
- Zones 6–9
- Sun, partial shade
- Sources: h, n, oo, aaa, fff

Attractive small shrub, easy to grow from seed. Bees love it. Leaves and edible flowers used in small quantities for tea.

bee balm

Monarda didyma 'Gardenview Scarlet'
- Perennial
- 3–4′
- Summer
- Aromatic foliage
- Rose red
- Zones 4–9
- Sun
- Sources: c, n

Moderate powdery mildew resistance. Attracts bees and hummingbirds. Keep compact by cutting back before flowering.

foxglove

Digitalis 'Excelsior'
- Biennial
- 5′
- Spring of 2nd year
- Pink with white and purple markings in throat
- Zones 4–10
- Part shade
- Sources: kk, uu, zz, bbb

Big tubular flowers with exotic inner markings. Self-sows, so it seems perennial. Digitalis is the source of the heart medicine.

lavender

Lavandula × intermedia 'Provence'
- Shrub
- To 3′
- Summer into fall
- Fragrant
- Mauve
- Sun
- Zones 5–10
- Sources: fff, iii, jjj

Also called lavandin. Numerous flower spikes. Is a variation of *L. x intermedia* 'Grosso'. Not for the hot, humid South.

breadseed poppy

Papaver somniferum

- Annual
- To 4'
- Summer
- White, pink, red, purple
- Sun
- Source: bbb

Lovely papery blossoms to 4" across. Seed capsules contain the black poppy seed used in cooking. Reseeds.

garden of plenty

Vegetables, herbs, and flowers grow and thrive in well-ordered profusion in this Minnesota garden on the edge of the wilderness in northern lake country. Their nurturing goodness satisfies the senses of all who visit Nelson's Resort, where the growing season is short but blessedly abundant. The promise of good fishing attracts guests, and the wholesome meals prepared with produce from the lodge's garden also lure them.

j

Jacque Eggen tends the land her grandmother Millie gardened, carved from the Minnesota wilderness at the edge of Crane Lake during the Depression. The plot is part of Nelson's Resort, a nationally-known family fishing retreat.

Jacque plans the garden on paper each year. To grow enough produce for resort-sized appetites in the short growing season of zone 3, she avoids ground-gobbling crops such as corn and potatoes. While heat-loving plants, such as melons, are out of the question, northern

Minnesota's cool summer nights are ideal for lettuce, which rarely bolts. Jacque relies on 'Romance' romaine lettuce, 'Reine des Glaces' Batavian, 'Red Salad Bowl' oakleaf, and 'Lollo Rossa' red looseleaf lettuce for plenty of fresh salads. 'Savoy King Hybrid' cabbage, one of Millie's old standbys, earns its place in the garden each year with crisp, leafy heads mild enough for salads and pretty enough for garnish.

Spring finds Jacque gathering piles of hazel brush from the woods for sugar snap peas to scale. Grandma Millie did the same years ago, preventing peas from rotting on the ground. Jacque starts 'Oregon Sugar Pod II' and 'Suprt Sugarmel' sugar snap peas in three successive plantings for multiple harvests, ensuring a fresh supply through the summer. Bush beans, lettuces, tomatoes, green peppers, cabbage, and cucumbers also produce quickly enough to yield several crops from staggered plantings. Specially-built cedar trellises encourage cucumber vines to climb up, saving space and making picking easy.

The garden's lushness is the heart of its beauty. Precisely-patterned plots neatly-mown paths keep the abundance orderly. When guests aren't out on the water, they're strolling through the garden or enjoying its rewards in the rustic dining room. For Jacque, it all comes naturally.

SHORT-SEASON GARDENING

Jacque Eggen gardens in zone 3, with a growing season of approximately 110 to 120 days. Water surrounds the resort on three sides, holding off frost a bit longer than for the surrounding area. Although it's difficult to grow certain plants, such as melons, there are advantages to this climate. Cool nights prolong the growing time for lettuce—it doesn't bolt as it does in warmer areas.

Recommended varieties for short-season gardens include 'Baby Spike' and 'Little Finger' carrots, 'Ace Hybrid' bell peppers, 'Savoy King Hybrid' cabbage, 'Romance', 'Nancy', 'Nevada', and 'Pirat' lettuce, 'Sweet Success' cucumber, 'Dwarf Blue Curled Vates' kale, and 'Olympia' spinach.

creating a **bountiful** garden

Siting a garden near water moderates the temperature. *Opposite:* Overview of the garden.

Jacque Eggen inherited a **green thumb** and a passion for gardening from her grandmother. From an early age, she helped in the garden and learned many techniques from Grandma Millie that she still uses today. Over the years, her interest and knowledge have increased, as have other demands on her time. She manages the resort hands-on, from hiring staff and scheduling reservations to buying for and maintaining the trading post. Nonetheless, the size of the garden has grown. And each year, Jacque grows hundreds of plants, all of them from seed. Grandma Millie would be proud.

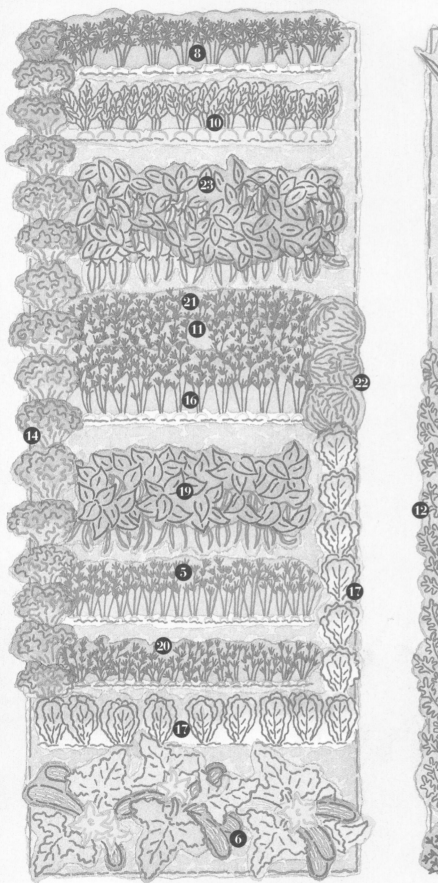
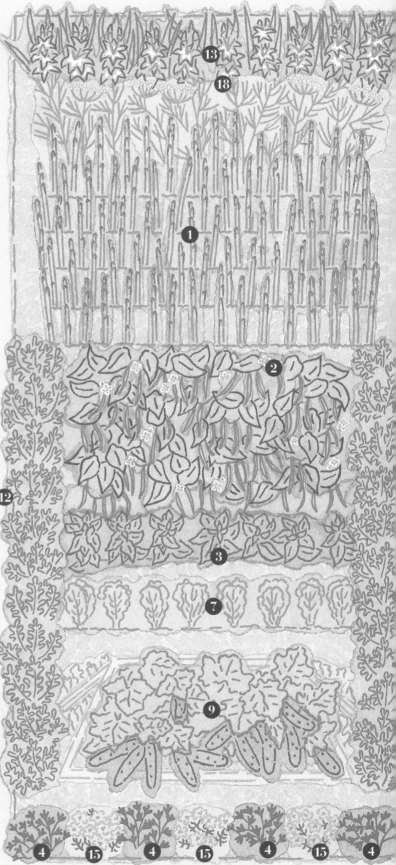

asparagus

Asparagus officinalis
- Perennial
- 3–5'
- Foliage plant
- Zones 4–10
- Sun
- Sources: h, m, o, w, uu

Usually grown from bare-root crowns. Takes effort to start a bed but worth it in most regions; does not do well in hot, humid climates.

bush bean

Phaseolus vulgaris 'Florence'
- Annual
- To 2'
- 50 days
- Summer harvest
- Sun
- Source: ddd

Early, dark green, flavorful pods. High-yielding, heat-tolerant, disease-resistant plants.

new zealand spinach

Tetragonia tetragonioides
- Annual
- 1–2', trailing
- Foliage plant
- Sun
- Sources: w, ff, aaa

Not a real spinach; has similar but stronger flavor and is used like spinach. More tolerant of warm weather than spinach.

italian broadleaf parsley

Petroselinum 'Catalogno'
- Biennial
- 12"
- 75 days
- White flowers 2nd year
- Zones 5–9
- Sun, partial shade
- Sources: h, w

Flat-leaf parsley with good flavor and vigorous growth. Great dried or fresh in stews, salads, and soups.

carrot

Daucus carota hyb.
- Biennial grown as annual
- 12"
- 72 days
- Flowers 2nd year
- White
- Sun
- Source: e

Carrots are not just orange; they are also white, red, purple, and yellow. 'Sweet Sunshine' is true yellow and extra-sweet.

zucchini

Cucurbita pepo 'Burpee Hybrid'
- Annual
- 24–30"
- 50 days

- Summer
- Yellow
- Sun
- Source: e

Medium green, flavorful summer squash. Compact, vigorous plants. Zucchini is best when picked young. Flowers are edible.

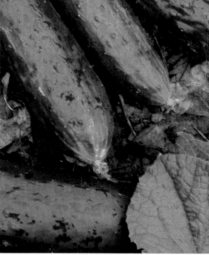

romaine lettuce

Lactuca sativa 'Balloon'
- Annual
- 10–12"
- 75+ days
- Harvest spring to fall
- Foliage plant
- Sun to partial shade
- Source: h

Large, pale, fine-textured romaine. Heat-tolerant. Excellent for Caesar salads.

cucumber

Cucumis sativus
'Parks All Season Burpless'
- Annual
- 4–5' vine
- 48–50 days
- Summer fruit
- Sun
- Source: ii

Completely burpless, sweet, crispy cukes. Heavy-bearing, vigorous, disease-resistant plants. Give cucumbers lots of water; fertilize with a balanced organic fertilizer.

parsnip

Pastinaca sativa
- Biennial grown as annual
- To 3'
- 95–120 days
- Grown for root
- Sun
- Sources: w, ff, ii, zz, ddd,

Needs well-drained soil without rocks to impede the taproot's growth. Harvest in the fall after a frost, which improves the flavor. Keeps well in a cool cellar or the refrigerator.

golden beet

Beta vulgaris
'Burpee's Golden'
- Biennial grown as annual
- To 12"
- 55 days
- Grown for foliage, roots
- Sun
- Sources: e, h, uu, xx

Delicious, very sweet, golden roots. Doesn't bleed when cooked like red beets do. Tops are good cooked as greens. Harvest several young leaves while root is growing.

carrot

Daucus carota hyb.
- Biennial grown as annual
- 6″
- Flowers 2nd year
- White
- Sun
- Sources: h, w, ff, ii, zz

Best flavor when grown during cool weather but can be grown in the summer. Likes rich, well-drained soil. Seeds must stay moist to germinate.

gladiola

Gladiolus hyb.
- Bulb
- 2–3′
- Summer
- White to purple
- Zones 7–10
- Sun
- Sources: e, ii, kk

Showy in the garden and as cut flowers; wide variety of colors. Dig up corms in fall in cold winter areas and store indoors. Stagger plantings for longer bloom.

oakleaf lettuce

Lactuca sativa 'Red Salad Bowl' ('Red Oakleaf')
- Annual
- 8–10″
- 51 days
- Harvest spring to fall
- Foliage plant
- Sun
- Sources: h, w, zz

Classic red oakleaf with deeply lobed leaves. Slow to bolt. Color is best in cool weather. Pick outer leaves as needed for salads.

looseleaf lettuce

Lactuca sativa 'Lollo Rossa'
- Annual
- 8–10″
- 45–60 days
- Foliage plant
- Sun
- Sources: h, w, zz,

Beautiful, deeply curled, magenta leaves. Very tasty. Grow as baby lettuce, a cut-and-come-again crop, or to maturity. Heat-tolerant.

signet marigold

Tagetes tenuifolia 'Tangerine Gem'
- Annual
- 8″
- Summer
- Orange
- Sun
- Sources: h, w, uu

Perfect in the edible garden; edible flowers have a better flavor than most marigolds. Remove the bitter white base of the petal before eating.

carrot

Daucus carota 'Belgium White'
- Biennial grown as annual
- 12″
- 75 days
- Flowers 2nd year
- White
- Sun

- Sources: d, qq

Heirloom; white inside and out with green shoulders. Best grown during cool weather.

romaine lettuce

Lactuca sativa
- Annual
- 10–12″
- 66–83 days
- Harvest spring to fall
- Sun to partial shade
- Sources: e, h, uu, w, ii

Tall, crispy, full-flavored leaves. Lettuce is most successful when seeds are started indoors and then transplanted into the garden.

dill

Anethum graveolens
- Annual, herb
- 36″
- Summer
- Aromatic foliage
- Yellow
- Sun
- Sources: e, ii, oo, fff

A must in summer gardens. Attracts butterflies and beneficial insects. Use for making pickles and enhancing many other foods.

yellow snap bean

Phaseolus vulgaris hyb.
- Annual
- To 2', bush
- 55–60 days
- Summer harvest
- Sun
- Sources: h, w, uu, zz, ddd

Has a delicate, mellow flavor. Sow directly in the garden after the soil has warmed. If birds are a problem, protect the seedbed with netting.

kuroda carrot

Daucus carota 'Coral II' ('Kurado Chantenay')
- Biennial grown as annual
- 12"
- 70–72 days
- Flowers 2nd year
- White
- Sun
- Sources: m, ss

From Japan. Deep, rich flavor; makes an exquisitely flavored juice. Large roots, strong, disease-tolerant tops.

carrot

Daucus carota 'Thumbelina'
- Biennial grown as annual
- 12"
- 51–65 days
- Flowers 2nd year
- White
- Sun
- Sources: e, m, w, ii, kk, ff, aaa

Small, round carrot. Great for soils too heavy for long carrots. Good flavor, crisp texture. Smooth skin that doesn't need peeling.

batavian lettuce

Lactuca sativa 'Reine des Glaces'
- Annual
- 10"
- 60–75 days
- Foliage plant
- Sun
- Source: h

Small heads with dark green, deeply cut, almost lacy leaves. Use as a leaf lettuce after the head is cut.

sugar snap pea

Pisum sativum
'Oregon Sugar Pod II'
- Annual
- 4' vines
- 64 days
- Spring
- White or purple
- Sun
- Sources: ff, aaa, ddd

Sweet, edible pods and peas. Likes cool weather and well-drained soil.

year-round harvest

a North Carolina kitchen garden dishes up effective landscape ideas, combining vegetables, flowers, and herbs in a design that is classic and inventive. In this gentle climate, the gardener fills the gathering basket every month of the year with okra, kale, pole beans, and bush beans. In this well-planned landscape, the design of the garden also is something to savor.

A sundial anchors one end of the garden, adding a note of formality. *Opposite*: Columnar apples.

the fresh flavor of the South keeps Genie White busy picking. From okra, bush beans, pole beans, tomatoes, eggplants, squash, cucumbers, and two kinds of peppers, to broccoli, carrots, and kale, her North Carolina garden yields harvests year-round. When the hot summer sun finally gives way to fall, it's time for leafy collard, turnip, and mustard greens. Even winter brings fresh spinach, lettuces, and spring onions.

The good taste doesn't stop with vegetables. With the help of landscape consultant Phyllis Herring, Genie weaves her love of flowers and family history into a garden to behold. An old millstone from the family farm takes center stage in an herb garden. Spiky-blossomed foxgloves mingle with herbs, while dwarf English boxwood borders beds with a touch of formality.

Food crops are surrounded by color, as roses ramble along fences and arbors. An arched entrance to the garden supports a cloak of roses, which bloom at will from spring until December. Lenten roses, an essential garden ingredient for Genie, take over where the roses left off, flowering from late January to April.

Fences, arbors, and paths give the garden structure. A mixture of paving materials adds texture and interest as one path yields to another. For herb-garden paths, Genie chose pea gravel. Herbs prefer good drainage, which the gravel provides, and tolerate the heat the paths absorb. Other footpaths combine brick and slate.

More than just a way to get from here to there, the pathways also direct views. Each glance inward is carefully composed, like a framed snapshot of a garden vignette.

Growing southern favorites doesn't keep Genie from looking for ideas from afar. A grid of standard apple trees—inspired by those at the Chelsea Flower Show in England—directs attention to a well-placed focal point in the far bed. There, an English saddle stone stands among a bed of annuals. Pastel pansies and forget-me-nots show off in spring, followed by drought-tolerant narrowleaf zinnias (*Zinnia angustifolia*) and drifts of dianthus. As if a reminder is needed of flavors among the glory, onions, greens, and pole beans grow nearby.

growing flavors and flowers

CREATING A KITCHEN GARDEN

A little bit of hard work at the outset will pay off in big rewards at harvest time. Start by developing a plan to prevent a lot of trial and error. Break up the garden with focal points; benches, sundials, sculptures, and arches provide year-round interest. Soften formal beds with vines, such as perennial sweet peas, clematis, and old climbing roses, tied to fences. Use ground covers and path materials for textural interest. Pea gravel is excellent for herb gardens. Use compost to amend soil. Rotate placement of vegetables yearly to help with pest control and soil conditioning. Pull greens and replant when they begin to bolt. Consider framing vegetable beds with perennials and annuals such as snapdragons, foxgloves, and *Petunia integrifolia*.

Slates make good paths between the garden beds. *Opposite:* Overview of the garden.

Genie incorporates family history into the landscape.

With a reverence for tradition, she has placed an antique millstone from her family's farm in Lancaster County, South Carolina, in the center of the herb garden. Atop the stone, which is outlined by dwarf boxwoods, is her grandmother's sundial, marking time during the growing season of the greens and vegetables nearby. With the help of landscape consultant Phyllis Herring, she has created a charming blend of useful and attractive plants, which yield a constant supply of produce for the table. The family eats all that they grow. But, Genie confesses, she would rather garden than cook.

1. Columnar Apple
2. Lamb's-Ears
3. Forget-Me-Not
4. Looseleaf Lettuce
5. Mustard Greens
6. Yellow Tomato
7. Japanese Mustard
8. Floribunda Rose
9. Purple Pole Bean
10. Bush Bean
11. Pansy
12. Hollyhock
13. Spanish Onion
14. Beets
15. Johnny-Jump-Up

lamb's ears

Stachys byzantina
(*S. lanata*)
* Perennial
* 3′
* Summer
* White and purple, pink
* Zones 4–9
* Sun
* Sources: c, s, iii

No insect pests, or even deer, care much for it. Too much water can rot the soft, felty leaves.

columnar apple

Malus 'Colonnade'
* Deciduous fruit tree
* 8′
* Spring
* White, pink

* Zones 4–8
* Sun
* Source: yy

Apple trees that grow in the shape of a column. Good for small spaces. Selection of cultivars that bear red, green, or golden full-size apples in September.

forget-me-not

Myosotis sylvatica
* Biennial
* 5–12″
* Spring, early summer
* Blue with yellow eyes
* Zones 5–9
* Partial shade
* Sources: zz, bbb

Happy little flowers that add a touch of blue to spring gardens. Prefers moist, well-drained soil. Reseeds.

looseleaf lettuce

Lactuca sativa
'Black-Seeded Simpson'
* Annual
* 8–12″
* 45
* Foliage plant

* Sun
* Sources: h, m, w, ff, kk, xx, zz, ddd

Heirloom with light green, frilled leaves around an almost-white center. Very tasty. Fast-growing, early, vigorous, and very popular.

mustard greens

Brassica juncea hyb.
* Annual
* To 2′
* 45–50 days
* Summer
* Yellow
* Sun
* Sources: h, w, ff, ss, aaa

Cool-season crop; grow as you would lettuce. Harvest a few leaves as you need them; served raw or cooked.

yellow tomato

Lycopersicon esculentum 'Gold Dust'
* Annual
* Semideterminate
* 60–65 days
* Summer harvest
* Sun
* Source: w

Orange-yellow skin and flesh with good flavor. Produces early and heavily; has good cold and heat tolerance.

japanese mustard

Brassica juncea
'Osaka Purple'
* Annual
* 12–14″
* 40 days
* Summer

* Yellow
* Sun
* Sources: h, w

Milder flavor than 'Giant Red'. Leaves are purple with white veins. Great for baby greens. Flowers are edible.

floribunda rose

Rosa 'Brass Band' ™
- Shrub, deciduous
- 36–48"
- Late spring-summer
- Golden apricot
- 7–9
- Sun
- Source: v

May be fashioned into a tree or standard rose by grafting onto long-stemmed stock. More tender than most.

bush bean

Phaseolus vulgaris 'Derby'
- Annual
- To 2'
- 57 days
- Summer harvest
- Sun
- Sources: zz, ddd

Extremely high yields of very tender green beans. Resistant to common bean mosaic. Plant seeds after the soil has warmed in spring.

purple pole bean

Phaseolus vulgaris hyb.
- Annual
- To 6'
- 55–70 days
- Harvest summer to frost
- Sun
- Sources: d, h, w, k, ff, uu

Purple pods are a color treat in the garden. They turn bright green after cooking. More tolerant of cold soil than green snap beans.

pansy

Viola × wittrockiana hyb.
- Perennial grown as annual
- 6–9"
- Spring, early summer
- White to purple
- Sun, partial shade
- Sources: ii, zz, bbb

Likes fertile, moist soil, cool weather, and afternoon shade in hot areas. Lovely draped over the edge of raised beds, in containers, or in mixed borders. Edible flowers have a mild minty flavor.

hollyhock

Alcea rosea
- Biennial
- 3–10'
- Summer
- White to purple
- Zones 3–10
- Sun
- Sources: tt, zz, bbb

Give plenty of sun and good air circulation to keep mildew and rust at bay. Keep water off the leaves when irrigating to reduce chance of rust.

beets

Beta vulgaris
- Biennial grown as annual
- To 12"
- 50-80 days
- Grown for foliage, roots
- Sun
- Sources: m, ff, uu, ddd, aaa

'Detroit Dark Red' is a classic heirloom; 'Cylindra' is great for slicing; try 'Long Season' for a good storage beet; 'Little Ball' is a baby beet, great for pickling.

spanish onion

Allium cepa 'White Sweet Spanish'
- Perennial, bulb
- 20–36"
- 105–130 days
- Fall harvest
- Zones 5–8
- Sun
- Sources: kk, zz

Mild, firm flesh. Long-day onion. Needs rich soil. Water, fertilize regularly. Seed indoors January-February, transplant early spring.

johnny-jump-up

Viola tricolor
- Perennial grown as annual
- 6–12"
- Spring, summer
- Purple, yellow, and white
- Sun, partial shade
- Zones 4–10
- Sources: w, ii

Prefers cool weather and moist, rich soil. Needs some sun to bloom well. Great in pots, hanging baskets, borders.

creating
your

kitchen

garden

a kitchen garden enhances a landscape—from the overall design of the garden and the beauty of the plants to the bountiful harvest it provides. The diversity of kitchen gardens across America, as seen on the preceding pages, gives you the inspiration to create your own. Once you've chosen one of the plans, the following pages will guide you through the planning process from the ground up—from the site and soil to the plants and ornaments that will make your garden unique.

When asked to picture a kitchen garden, many people think of their grandmother's gardens or the Victory gardens of World War II. They were gardens of necessity, based on a need to produce a family's food—enough to eat fresh and preserve for the winter.

Strictly speaking, these were not kitchen gardens, but vegetable gardens laid out as a series of rows. They had no element of design, and were often a large square or rectangle. A kitchen garden, on the other hand, combines both form and function, beauty and practicality.

Vegetable gardens have straight rows with soldier-like plantings. They are practical as well as easy to plant and maintain.

Thomas Jefferson's garden at Monticello, Virginia, was designed in this fashion. Although it covered over two acres and contained over a thousand different plants, the plan was similar, only larger. The garden was broken into 24 squares that were planted according to the part of the plant destined for harvest.

The geometric design and symmetry of this garden is emphasized by the brick paths.

The First Kitchen Gardens

Kitchen gardens are popular today, yet they date back several thousand years. The exact date of the first kitchen garden is unknown, but the first step toward a kitchen garden came when a tree was purposely planted with other edibles. From records of an early Chinese herbal, we know that medicinal herb gardens were cultivated as early as the third millennium B.C.

By 2700 B.C., Egyptians had recorded growing over 500 herbs.

A Sumerian legend from the same era tells of a goddess who fell in love with a gardener. His garden had trees planted in the corners, creating shade and shelter. The enclosed area contained trained vines, vegetables in rows, and a water source or feature.

A small Egyptian painting in the British Museum, dated circa 1400 B.C., shows the garden of Nebamun. It is rectangular with a suggestion of a stone border. In the pond, there are waterfowl, flowers, and fish. Date palms form a symmetrical pattern around the pond.

In the ancient Middle East, pleasure gardens were beautiful yet practical. Walls protected the house from marauders and warmed the gardens. Buffered by the walls, exotic plants that would not normally grow could thrive. A pond in the center of the garden was a source of water for the garden and a home to fish that were raised as food for the table.

Medieval Gardens

Several documents dating back to the reign of Charlemagne (about 800 A.D.) describe gardens of the era. From the perspective of kitchen gardens, the most significant is the plan for a Swiss monastery. Four rectangular gardens, each with its own purpose, were laid

a brief **history** of kitchen gardens

Boxwood balls or small boxwood hedges delineate the edge of a garden bed.

out within a square cloister. The physic garden (medicinal herb garden), which was located close to the infirmary, had 16 separate planting beds. The vegetable garden was made up of 18 beds laid out in two rows of nine. Yet another garden featured fruit trees planted symmetrically.

Medieval gardens shared specific details: They were either square or rectangular. A wall or fence (often a high wattle fence) enclosed the garden. Crossing paths bisected each garden, dividing each into more similarly shaped beds or gardens. This design formed the basis for all of the formal gardens later developed in Europe.

Persian Gardens

The gardens of Persia (modern-day Iran) were designed in direct response to the climate. Persia was a level, barren, and arid plain, baked by fierce sun most of the year. The garden was a sanctuary from the elements, with intensive gardening and a place to enjoy nature instead of challenging it. The paradise gardens, as they were called, were enclosed, fertile, and laden with fruit and flowers. At the center was a pool, pond, or a fountain. Streams crossing in the center bisected the garden.

Such garden designs are depicted in the great Persian garden carpets. They show several borders of trees and flowers. The garden itself is divided into four parts by rivers, with a circular design in the center—a foursquare design with the rivers forming a symbolic cross. Persian and Islamic design influences continue today.

A variation of the foursquare garden still maintains the pattern's symmetry.

English Foursquare Gardens

Early English kitchen gardens were based on the same foursquare layout. But in this venue, the garden was divided into four rectangular plots by two intersecting paths, not by waterways. This simple design provided an ease of culture where herbs, vegetables, grains, and fruit could all be grown together. It also created a rich yet unpretentious display of color and form. Even in times of dire need, some flowers crept into the garden to add a touch of beauty.

Symmetry often gave way to practicality— paths were offset when required. Allowances were made for doors, windows, or entrances.

A wall of some sort enclosed the garden. These were the forerunners of the modern outdoor "room." As in the gardens that preceded them, the walls were functional, protecting the garden, creating a warmer microclimate in which to grow a wider range of edibles. Originally, the gate was a practical part of the design, forming the entryway into the garden (through the wall). Today, it's more of a design element, giving the garden a distinct style.

Kitchen Gardens— Today and Tomorrow

The kitchen garden of today is driven as much by aesthetics as by necessity. Beautiful vegetables are combined with herbs, annual and perennial flowers, and fruit in creative ways. Those of the future will be similar; the only difference will be the varieties that will be grown. Throughout its long history, the kitchen garden pleases the eye as much as the palate.

Loam crumbles a bit after being squeezed. The dark color is a clue to its richness.

In order to grow and thrive, plants need sun, water, and nutrients. An area that gets at least six hours of

getting started—at soil level

sun a day is the best site for a kitchen garden. In fact, most vegetables benefit from more sun—except in the hot South, where selective shading in summer is useful.

Natural rainfall may be enough water for some plants, but most vegetables benefit from supplemental watering. There are many ways to provide plants with water—both low-tech and high-tech. In a small garden, a simple watering can or hose-end sprinkler is often the simplest way to water. A computerized, in-ground irrigation system represents the opposite end of the spectrum.

Soil Structure

Soil is the seemingly magic substrate that anchors plants in place and supplies many of their nutritional needs. Yet many novice gardeners seem most intimidated by soil.

Instead of being intimidated, put your common sense—and a very basic knowledge of soil science—to work.

Sand, like the sand at the beach, has a very loose structure—water runs right through it. Clay, on the other hand, retains water. The same holds true for sandy and clay soil.

The type of soil your garden has is determined by the relative amounts of sand, clay, and silt the soil actually contains. The best soils have some sand, some silt, and a little clay. Referred to as loams, these soils hold nutrients, drain adequately, and are easy to work with. They are loose enough for roots to easily penetrate.

Know Your Soil

Different areas of the country have distinct soil types. There are two simple, do-at-home tests to determine the physical properties of your soil.

The easiest and quickest is called the squeeze test. Take a handful of slightly moist garden soil and gently squeeze it. Open your hand and look at the soil. Sandy soil won't hold any shape. It crumbles and falls easily through your fingers. Clay forms a tight ball, retaining the squeeze marks. Loam is between sand and clay. It seems to conform to your hand's shape and is a ball, yet it's crumbly on the edges.

The second way to determine your soil type is the jar method. Combine ½ cup of soil with 1½ cups of water in a glass jar. Cover the jar and shake vigorously. Shake it enough to loosen up the soil and get it moving through the water. The soil components will settle out in different ways. Sand settles quickly to the bottom of the jar—measure its height after one minute. Silt is the next to settle on top of the sand. Measure its height after one hour. The final component, clay, settles on top of the silt. Measure it after one day. If the layers of silt and sand are the same size as the layer of clay, you have good loamy

Good loamy soil is the key element to a successful kitchen garden.

Large branches from a fallen tree make a good structure for a compost pile.

soil. Some experts suggest that the best loam is about 20 percent clay and 40 percent each silt and sand. If you have more sand, then it is a sandy loam.

Improving Soil

If you don't have perfect soil, don't despair—you can improve your soil by adding organic matter. Leaf mold, compost, and well-rotted manure are the best amendments for improving soil structure.

Add soil amendments when preparing the garden for planting. They are also useful as top dressings to spread around plants growing in the garden. They act as both a mulch and a slow-release fertilizer.

Organic mulches, such as pinestraw and cocoa and barley hulls, break down over time and benefit the soil.

No-Dig Gardening

Digging and rototilling can overwork the soil. By constantly working the soil, there is the danger of its structure breaking down into a dust-like powder or hardening like concrete.

Many gardeners never rototill or turn their soil. Instead, they prepare their beds in the fall for spring planting by spreading as much as 12 inches of organic matter over the beds. Any organic matter, such as compost, hay, oak leaves (shredded are best), sawdust, pine

needles, shredded newspaper, manure, vegetable scraps, and peat moss will work. Moisten the whole area, add a little agricultural lime and wait for it to break down. The soil is easily worked the next spring; simply push the mulch aside and plant your seeds or seedlings. Continuously replenish the mulch, and the soil will get better and better. This approach also saves time-consuming weeding.

It is important to not dig or work the soil when it is too dry or too wet. In spring, use the squeeze test to determine if the soil is ready to be worked. If the soil forms a loose ball that falls apart when poked, it's safe to dig or plant.

Black Gold— Compost

Compost is decomposed organic matter, usually derived from fruit and vegetable scraps, grass clippings, garden cuttings, leaves, eggshells, sawdust, weeds (without seeds), coffee grounds, and shredded newspaper.

Compost happens—it just takes time for the material to break down. Although there are many formulas for the ratio of brown (dried, such as fall leaves) to green (fresh, such as grass trimmings, vegetable scraps), as long as the pile gets enough air and moisture, it will decompose and turn into black gold.

The process can be as simple as piling the ingredients in a corner of the yard, or adding them to a $300 compost tumbler. The pile will take longer to decompose than the tumbler that is turned daily. A compost bin is easy to make out of metal fencing, wooden pallets, cement blocks, or wood. Commercially available models are made of plastic or metal; some rotate to speed up the process.

Leaf Mold

Leaf mold, which is simply composted leaves, is a good soil amendment—and it is easy to make. After raking leaves in fall, run the lawn mower over them to break them into smaller pieces. Pile these into a 3- by 3-foot bin. Wet the leaves every so often, turn them over a few times (optional), and within a year you'll have a finished pile.

The Acid Test

pH is a measure of relative acidity or alkalinity. It determines whether nutrients in the soil are available to plants. pH is measured on a scale of 1 to 14, with a pH of 7.0 considered neutral. Most plants perform best in soils with a pH level between 6.0 and 7.5.

The best way to determine your soil's pH is to have the soil tested. Contact your local Cooperative Extension Service for information. In most areas, you can take soil samples to their office, and they will perform the test for a nominal fee. Make certain they also provide suggestions for changing the soil pH when needed.

Correcting pH Problems

Acid soil (soil with a low pH) is the most common problem gardeners encounter. To raise the pH one full point—from 5.6 to 6.6—apply dolomitic limestone at the rate of 20 pounds per 1,000 square feet to sandy soil, 40 pounds to loamy soil, and 60 pounds for clay soil. Mix it into the soil with a compost fork. Retest the soil after about four months to determine the pH change.

Lowering the pH of alkaline soil is more difficult. An application of elemental sulfur will help, but the results vary by type of soil. Even if you are successful, the results will last only a few years. Instead, choose plants suited to alkaline soil, or grow your kitchen garden in raised beds.

keeping up with the needs of plants

Fertilizers, by the Numbers

Every fertilizer package has three numbers printed on it, whether it is an organic, inorganic, or chemical fertilizer. These numbers, such as 20-20-20, represent the N-P-K ratio—the percentage of those specific macronutrients. A 100-lb. bag labeled 5-10-5 contains the following: 5 lbs. of nitrogen (N), 10 lbs. of phosphorus (P), and 5 lbs. of potassium (K).

Water

Water is critical to all life. Plants generally are more than 90 percent water and need a steady supply to perform their best. Vegetables need proper moisture levels from seedling stage through harvest.

Soil texture determines how deeply water penetrates. In sandy soil, 1 inch of water on the surface will moisten roots to 12 inches deep. In clay soil, that same 1 inch of water will only go 4 to 5 inches deep. You can measure the amount of water plants get from sprinklers or rainfall by using a container or a rain gauge.

The frequency of watering depends on several factors. Sandy soils or hot, sunny locations need more water than clay soils or shady spots. Weather also changes plants' needs for water. Plants in cloudy or cool conditions demand less water than those in hot and sunny areas. Some crops need more water than others do. Leafy vegetables need more water than root vegetables.

Watering

Whenever you water, soak the root systems of plants thoroughly. For seedlings or young plants, that means soaking to a depth of only a few inches. Deep-rooted plants will need soaking to a much greater depth.

Although sprinklers and hoses can provide lots of summer fun, they are not the best choice for watering vegetables, herbs, and flowers—a kitchen garden. You can easily and inexpensively install drip irrigation systems—some have timers and computerized controls. Special emitters release water gradually to individual plants, so the water can slowly soak into the soil.

A weepy hose or leaky pipe hose slowly leaks water from all sides. Lay it down around larger plants or between rows. Keep the hose uncovered or bury it beneath a two-inch layer of mulch.

Sprinklers are portable and easily placed. However, much water is lost to evaporation with a sprinkler—the water goes on the plant, not necessarily down at soil level where the roots are. Water early in the morning so the leaves will dry off in the warmth of the sun. Late-day watering promotes fungus and disease, as leaves remain wet all night.

Furrow watering is not commonly done, but it is a good way to irrigate perennial plantings, such as asparagus. This type of watering works only on level ground in soil that is not sandy. Design the garden with furrows between the raised beds. To work well, the raised areas should be no more than four feet across, and the furrows one foot wide and six inches deep. Slowly flood the furrows, then dam off a section to allow the water to penetrate.

Drip irrigation puts water at soil level where roots can use it.

Mulch

Mulch is any material spread on the soil to prevent weeds from growing. Mulch also keeps soil temperatures from fluctuating and helps retain soil moisture. Many plants benefit with a thick layer of mulch at their roots, which prevents soil-born diseases from splashing on the leaves. Using as much as six inches of organic mulch at the base of tomato plants, for example, prevents many diseases.

Organic mulch breaks down, becomes part of, and improves the soil. Shredded newspaper, leaves, grass clippings (add it an inch at a time, or it will become slimy and not break down), straw, well-rotted manure, and compost allow water to penetrate and help control weeds.

Locally plentiful organic mulches are often the best choice—they are less expensive (sometimes free for the taking). Many cities and towns now have composting programs and make the compost available to residents. Utility companies and municipalities also make wood chips available to residents. Depending on where you live, you may be able to get cocoa hulls, buckwheat hulls, ground corn cobs, peanut hulls, pecan hulls, pine needles, salt hay, sawdust, straw, or wood shavings. All freshly processed wood by-products, such as bark, sawdust, and wood shavings, rob nitrogen from the top layer of soil as they begin to decay. Either compost them first or compensate by adding nitrogen fertilizer.

Black plastic sheeting helps warm the soil in spring and gives you a head start on planting. It is especially useful for heat-loving crops like melons. Spread it out and cut holes where you want to plant seedlings. Just realize that black plastic sheeting smothers the soil and doesn't allow water to penetrate. Provide irrigation to plants with a drip system or a soaker hose placed underneath the plastic.

Site Considerations

almost all fruits and vegetables like growing in full sun, so site a kitchen garden where it receives a minimum of six hours of sunlight each day. Don't assume that the area is totally sunny. Go out and look at it at different times of the day. If you're planning the garden in winter, be aware that the garden may seem sunny, but if there are deciduous trees nearby, the garden could be shaded when the trees leaf out. Also note

planning your garden lets you make the best use of your time and space. It is often best to start small, plan carefully, and maintain that space well for a season. Then you can decide how much more (or less) space you want to devote to the garden next season.

into the garden to harvest a fresh vegetable or snip an herb for a meal in progress. A nearby site will get much more use. Moreover, a well-used garden will produce the greatest satisfaction.

The site should be free of competing roots from trees and shrubs that

Plant Hardiness and Frost Dates

before sitting down to make a garden plan, it's important to know your limits and the limits of the climate

Map on page 151 shows the 11 hardiness zones for North America. Find your zone, then make sure the trees, shrubs, and perennials you buy are hardy in that zone.

Within any property, there are microclimates. If your kitchen garden has a wall around it, it may be a zone warmer than the rest of the property. An exposed area, on the other hand, may be a zone colder. Use the microclimates to your advantage to grow more and varied plants.

When planning the garden, it also helps to know when the last frost date is in spring and the first frost date in autumn.

making a plan for your kitchen garden

Remember that even with labor-saving approaches, each square foot of space added to the plan means more work in the garden.

shade from shrubs, buildings, fences, or other structures.

A location near the kitchen is ideal. The cook can then easily pop

would steal nutrients. Vegetables need frequent watering, so a source of water should be nearby. A spigot at the edge of the garden is ideal, though a site reachable with a length or two of hose will work.

where you live. A kitchen garden has a broader scope than the typical vegetable garden, with fruit trees, shrubs, and perennials These plants will remain in the garden for many years, unlike most vegetables, which are grown as annuals.

When buying permanent plants— anything besides annuals—knowing your hardiness zone helps you purchase plants that will survive your winter. The USDA Hardiness Zone

The USDA Plant Hardiness Zone Map of North America

Range of Average Annual Minimum Temperatures for Each Zone

ZONE 1 BELOW -50° F
ZONE 2 -50° TO -40°
ZONE 3 -40° TO -30°
ZONE 4 -30° TO -20°
ZONE 5 -20° TO -10°
ZONE 6 -10° TO   0°
ZONE 7   0° TO 10°
ZONE 8   10° TO 20°
ZONE 9   20° TO 30°
ZONE 10 30° TO 40°
ZONE 11 ABOVE 40°

Knowing your zone's frost dates allows you to get an early start in spring and to plan for a late harvest before fall. Many greens and some brassicas (kale, broccoli, and cabbage, for example) can take a light frost.

Grow What You'll Eat

Most modern kitchen gardens aren't the subsistence gardens of yesteryear. Today, people want much more from a garden. They want an attractive garden and the produce, but they don't have the time or space a large vegetable garden demands.

Start by determining what you want to eat. Consider growing some of the more uncommon or costly vegetables and fruits that you enjoy. Some gardeners want a salad garden and are happy to step outside the kitchen door to harvest a variety of greens, tomatoes, radishes, scallions, and baby carrots. Others want fresh vegetables and herbs during the entire summer. The largest garden will provide harvests all season long and have a surplus for preserving for future use. Plan staggered plantings for small harvests all season.

Add some flowers— edible or ornamental varieties—and you have the beginnings of a garden that is lovely and fruitful.

Drawing the Plan

Make a sketch of your garden using graph paper. This will help you estimate the amount of seed or plants you need to produce your desired harvest. Take it with you into the garden when you are planting. It's also interesting to compare yearly changes in your garden plan.

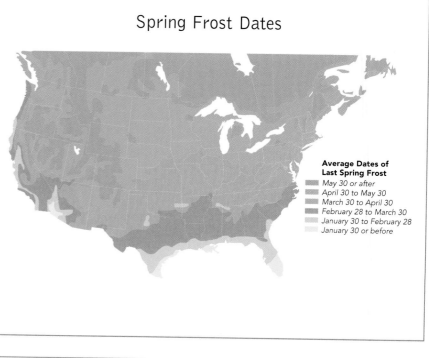

Spring Frost Dates

Average Dates of Last Spring Frost
- May 30 or after
- April 30 to May 30
- March 30 to April 30
- February 28 to March 30
- January 30 to February 28
- January 30 or before

Autumn Frost Dates

Average Dates of First Autumn Frost
- June 30 to July 30
- July 30 to August 30
- August 30 to September 30
- September 30 to October 30
- October 30 to November 30
- November 30 to December 30

almost everything you grow in a kitchen garden can be grown from seed. There are some notable exceptions, of course. French tarragon doesn't produce seed and must be grown from cuttings. And you might not want to wait for an apple tree to reach fruiting size from a seed.

There continues to be a great debate as to the best type of seed to grow—hybrid or heirloom. Decide for yourself what will be best in your garden.

Hybrids

more than a hundred years ago, Gregor Mendel, a monk, discovered the laws of inheritance through experiments with sweet peas. That knowledge, combined with a need to feed the world more efficiently, pushed scientists and plant breeders to develop new varieties of plants.

Commercial plant breeders develop hybrid plants to fulfill specific needs. They breed a sweet corn that all matures on the same date for more efficient harvesting. A tomato is hybridized with a skin hard enough to withstand shipping over thousands of miles. Plants are developed to produce much higher yields per acre.

Satisfying these requirements benefits commercial producers of vegetables and society as a whole. But the home gardener is usually more interested in flavor of fruits and vegetables and in color.

Heirlooms

in truth, heirlooms lack a precise definition. Some authorities believe that heirloom varieties must have been grown for over 50 years. In general, any cultivar or garden variety that has been passed from generation to generation is an heirloom. Some

believe the variety must have stayed in the same family, cherished and preserved by them through many generations. Others eliminate any that have been in commercial production.

Heirlooms are referred to as open-pollinated, suggesting that the fertilization of the female is done by a similar male (as opposed to a different one, as in a hybrid). Pollination takes place in the open field instead of in a controlled environment.

Heirlooms have a broad-based genetic diversity. In Darwin's language, they are the winners in the ongoing battle for survival of the fittest. These varieties have consistent qualities that are passed down from generation to generation.

Hybrids vs. Heirlooms

plant performance is measured in many ways. Some considerations include flavor, appearance, disease and insect resistance, uniformity, maturation time, yield, water and nutrient requirements, vigor, and storage and shipping qualities. Commercial hybrids usually have the edge when comparing uniformity, yield, and shipping qualities.

Home gardeners don't consider these qualities to be very important. They want only a small amount for the table and transport the bounty only a few steps, from the garden to the kitchen. They can choose a more flavorful variety whose skin easily bruises; flavor is what counts. The home gardener can plant a particularly flavorful

 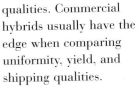

Heirloom varieties of flowers and vegetables are prized for their fragrance and flavor.

It's easy to save dill seeds. Use the seeds as a spice or save them to sow next year.

sweet corn that matures erratically, bearing enough ears for the family's dinner rather than all being picked at once and shipped to market. Heirlooms satisfy unusual taste preferences rather than pleasing the majority of shoppers.

Difficult Growing Conditions

ost hybrids are bred to perform consistently under intense cultivation techniques. Home gardeners can select varieties that perform best in their own growing conditions. High altitude, short seasons, limited water, or low fertility can be handled with careful selection of varieties. Many of the open-pollinated varieties have withstood the test of time and performed well under specific difficult conditions, many without the use of fungicides or insecticides. Just consider the number of years some of the hybrids have been grown, and they still perform well with little or no fuss.

Romancing The Seed

ome families are lucky enough to have their own heirloom varieties. Their immigrant ancestors may have carried the seed during the long and arduous trip from the old country. Family members who can recount the history through oral tradition, continue to grow the plant in their new homeland.

A number of heirloom varieties are associated with particular ethnic and cultural groups or indigenous peoples and have been maintained by those communities through many generations of gardeners. With a little research, a gardener may find that an heirloom was a staple part of a community's diet or as important as a ceremonial or feast crop.

With the growth in popularity of cooking ethnic specialties, heirloom varieties add a substantial note of authenticity to the

'Rainbow Lights Swiss' chard is a flavorful and colorful heirloom.

exercise. The history of the variety adds to both the gardener's and cook's pleasure and satisfaction.

Perhaps the strongest argument for growing heirloom varieties is the interesting stories about these plants. You have to wonder if long ago a farmer actually saved his homestead because of a bumper crop of 'Mortgage Lifter' tomatoes. How did the Czechoslovakian variety 'Eros' receive its name? And what are the stories that lie behind these tomatoes: 'Glacier', 'Glamour', 'Hawaiian', 'Mars', 'Mountain Princess', 'Silvery Fir Tree', 'Valley Girl', and 'Whippersnapper'?

Unusual Tastes and Colors

eirlooms offer a substantial range of color, taste, and shape from which to choose. The striped beet 'Chioggia', spotted lettuce 'Freckles', 'Belgium White' carrots, and 'Purple de Milpa' tomatillo are but a few examples. Heirloom tomatoes are more than just red beefsteaks. They come in yellow, white, purple, green, and stripes. They may be shaped like pears, grapes, marbles, or pumpkins. Some are even hollow—perfect for stuffing.

Safety in Biodiversity

The issue of heirlooms has become politicized and is a very hot topic. Many heirloom growers consider themselves the good guys pitched in battle against hybrid-loving agribusiness. Although the debate is complex, most people will agree that there is safety in maintaining biodiversity.

Large monocultural farming presents risks. The Irish potato famine occurred when a single disease wiped out the entire crop of that country's staple. With a diversified genetic base, such as exists in South America where potatoes are native, this would never have happened.

But it could happen again. As recently as 1970, corn was similarly affected. Corn blight destroyed over 15 percent of the entire harvest. A single gene had been used to breed most of the commercial corn varieties, making the crop an easy target for disease. Many other crops are also in danger.

But amazingly, there has been no wake-up call to gardeners or farmers. More than 45 percent of heirloom varieties available in 1984 are no longer offered in catalogs.

The good news is that a number of private and nonprofit seed trusts are working with networks of interested gardeners to grow and maintain these varieties. Seed Savers Exchange is one of the best-known. Each year they send people to Europe, Asia, and Africa to rescue seeds. With all the war and strife in the ever-changing political map of the world, one of the least publicized losses is that of genetic diversity in food crops. It's not the big wars; it's the battles fought on the home front. Villages are burned, lives are lost, and in the process, small home gardens are destroyed. And with their destruction, there is the loss of the seeds that have been saved and passed on by generations of people.

Growing these Italian heirloom vegetables allows you to plant a taste of the past.

Seed Saving

Gardeners get involved in the seed-saving process for many reasons. Some gardeners like the feeling of self-reliance that seed saving generates. This simple involvement in the process helps to conserve natural and agricultural resources.

Open-pollinated, nonhybrid varieties have seed that will grow into the same plant next season. Gardeners who want to get involved in the selection process can save seed of hybrids that will produce a range of offspring. Then they make selections based on preferred characteristics and begin to stabilize the plant. This is a complex and interesting challenge for some gardeners.

Most gardeners don't have ideal growing conditions—the soil may be too sandy, lacking nutrients, or perhaps it is clay. Whatever the soil in nutrients, or is very alkaline, it may be easier to switch than to fight. Instead of spending years amending the existing soil with organic matter, or getting frustrated trying to change the pH level, spend a weekend making a new garden by constructing raised beds.

gardening in raised beds

problem, it can be solved by making raised beds atop the problem site. Gardeners can create their ideal growing situation for whatever type of plant they want to grow.

Raised beds are an effective way to deal with poor soil. If your soil drains poorly, is low

Mounds

a simple way to create raised beds is to mound up the soil. Create elevated growing beds 6 to 12 inches above the ground. The top of the mound should measure approximately 3 feet wide, increasing to about 4 feet wide at ground level. This is a comfortable width— most people can easily reach into and work the beds from the sides or paths without stepping on the soil. Allow enough room for permanent paths between the beds. Before

constructing the mounds, loosen the soil several inches below the surface. You can add organic matter, topsoil, manure, and other amendments. Combine with a spading fork, thoroughly mixing all of the components. Shape the mounds with a rake by pulling in soil from the paths. In effect, you are raising the beds by lowering the paths. They will settle over several days, so wait a week or so to plant. If you plant in them right away, your plants also will sink over time.

Structured Sides

You can build deeper raised beds with large planter boxes from 1 to 3 feet high. Because of their depth, they need to have strong, permanent sides.

Build the sides with material that won't break down in a couple of years. Use railroad ties, old construction timbers, logs, cement blocks, or brick. Weather-resistant wood, such as cedar, lasts for many years. Avoid using wood treated with CCA or other chemicals for use with edibles.

The ideal width for a

tall raised bed is 4 feet. The length can vary to suit the style or design of the garden. To keep the sides stable, install wooden stakes at 2-foot intervals inside the wooden sides. Overlap the corners and reinforce them with 4×4s.

Garden soil is too heavy to use in the beds. Mix equal parts peat moss, compost, and topsoil. If this seems too heavy, add some perlite. Fill the beds to within 2 inches of the top, and water well.

Intensive Gardening

raised beds and mounds are ideal for the French intensive gardening method. It uses extra-rich organic soil, and plants are closely spaced. Rather than plant in straight rows, zigzag the placement. This method works whether you're growing ornamentals or vegetables.

Brick edging supports the raised bed and helps warm soil in spring.

Container gardening allows the most expression of style in a limited space. Some containers are small enough to be portable and add spot color as needed—in any season, in any location—in a kitchen garden. Place pots of flowering annuals or herbs wherever they're needed to create excitement.

rarely break. Many new and attractive colors and textures of plastic pots are now on the market.

Concrete and wooden containers are available in many sizes. One of the most common is the half whiskey barrel. Personalize a barrel by painting it in vivid (or muted) colors.

Look for different containers at garden centers—strawberry jars or hypertufa troughs. Almost anything can become a garden

A patio tower is ideal for those with limited space. It's great for a small salad garden.

mix that holds moisture but isn't soggy. It's easy to make your own potting soil by mixing equal parts compost, perlite, peat moss, and topsoil. Or purchase a

Watering

One of the facts of life of container gardening is that containers need frequent attention and

Plant Selection and Design Choices

When combining more than one type of plant in a container, there are a few design ideas to keep in mind. Use a tall, upright plant to give height to the planting.

add pizzazz with # containers

Choosing a Container

There are many types, sizes, and colors of containers. Choose a container with a drainage hole. Go for a large pot—fill it with several plants—as it won't dry out as quickly as small ones.

Terra-cotta pots are classic and look good in most situations. However, they are heavy, relatively expensive, breakable, and they dry out quickly. Plastic pots are lighter weight, relatively inexpensive, and they

container—a hollowed out log or tree trunk, wicker basket (lined with plastic sheeting), old boot, wooden shoes, wheelbarrow, or a child's red wagon.

Potting Mix and Fertilizer

Because containers tend to dry out quickly, you want a soil

soilless mix and add compost.

Mix in a slow-release granular fertilizer before planting. Use a water-soluble fertilizer once a week at half strength. If rain has been heavy or watering is frequent, fertilize more frequently.

watering. In hot weather, some may require daily watering (even twice daily in hot, dry climates). Add a two-inch layer of mulch on top of the soil to conserve moisture. If the growing mix dries out completely, put the pot in a larger container of water. Leave it for several hours until the water is absorbed.

Drape vines or creeping plants, such as thyme or creeping rosemary, over the edges of the container to soften the edges and make the planting more cohesive.

Mix textures, using soft-textured plants for filler. Plan the container as you would a border or garden. Decide on a theme or color palette. Other choices will follow naturally.

An old tire (cut, turned inside out, and painted) is a fun container for lettuce.

Herbs are rarely bothered by pests. The oniony scent of chives deters rabbits.

Many people first choose to garden organically (without chemicals) when they start raising edibles. Although research indicates that homeowners in general use far more pesticides per acre than farmers, some gardeners choose to eliminate or reduce the use of pesticides and inorganic fertilizers in their gardens. They become organic gardeners.

The benefits of going organic are many, such as fresh produce that is totally free of any residual chemicals. Some want to create a balanced ecosystem in their backyard.

A Fine Balance

When choosing to plant a garden without chemicals, you are striving for a balance with nature. You learn to tolerate the less-than-perfect-looking tomato, ear of corn, or squash. There may be some pests in the garden, but you can live with them. The basis of organic gardening is paying attention to details and all-around good gardening practices.

Preventing Problems

The first priority of every gardener is to build rich, organic-based soil that has a good structure. A good soil, sanitation, rotation, and companion planting are all helpful in preventing pests and diseases.

One of the keys to organic gardening is prevention. Plants stressed by lack of water and too much or too little sun are much more susceptible to diseases and pests. Diseases and pests rarely attack healthy, strong growing plants. Plan your garden so that plants get the amount of sun they need to thrive. Ensure adequate water supplies for your crops.

Great soil is another key to successful organic gardening. Good soil supports strong and healthy plants. Start with the best soil, rich in organic matter and with good tilth and texture. Improve the soil before planting and each succeeding year.

A neat garden, with debris picked up and no fruit left to rot on the vine, is generally a healthier garden than a messy one. Remove diseased plants, debris, and weeds from the garden site. In the fall, remove all plants killed by frost. Pull up the dead tomato plants, beans, and decaying vegetables and place all nondiseased material in the compost pile. Put a fresh layer of mulch over the entire area.

Pests and Disease

Sometimes, despite all care, a pest or disease presents itself in the garden. One way to avoid this is to examine every plant carefully before it goes into the ground. Never add a diseased, pest-infected plant, or a plant that just does not look healthy to your garden.

If a plant develops substantial disease or pest problem, simply throw it away (do not compost it) so the problem doesn't spread to other healthy plants in the garden.

explore the organic approach

Herbs

Many herbs, such as sage, repel insects from other plants. Deer avoid herbs, too.

Control insect problems by spotting them early. First identify the insect that is causing the problem. Then find the least toxic way to deal with it. Some insects can be hand-picked off plants. A hard spray of water from the hose early in the day will often control mites, aphids, and whiteflies. Think of it as the insect equivalent to a tidal wave—it knocks most of them right off the plant and drowns others.

If the problem recurs, try spraying with insecticidal soap or summer-weight horticultural oil. Remember though, that these solutions are not selective—they'll kill the good bugs as well as the bad bugs. If the pest still persists, use an organically derived insecticide such as pyrethrin. Whatever products you use, follow the label instructions. Treat them as you would any poisonous substance.

Crop Rotation

A simple way to avoid problems is to rotate crops in the garden. This can easily be done in any size garden and may be most important in a small garden. Keeping the same type of plant in the same area year after year invites diseases and pests to gain a foothold. Specific nutrients are depleted from the soil. Some soilborne diseases can remain in the soil for several years. If the same types of plants are grown in the same location, they will become very susceptible to disease. Do not plant the same type of crop in that area for at least three years. Some insects lay eggs in the soil near their favorite host plant. By rotating the host plant to a new location, the insect must work much harder. The final reason for crop rotation is to help balance nutrient needs

with what is available in the soil. Heavy feeders—plants with high nutrient needs, such as squash, tomatoes, and corn—should be grown in a location that had soil-building plants last season. All of the legumes (all types of beans, peanuts, peas, and soybeans) will help add nutrients to the soil. The next season, use that spot for light-feeding plants, such as carrots, garlic, peppers, potatoes, or Swiss chard.

Solarization

If soilborne disease is a chronic problem, remedy it by solarizing the soil during the hottest part of summer. Soak the area with water and cover it with sheets of clear plastic weighted on the edges with bricks. In six weeks, the soil heats up to a temperature that kills off pathogens.

Colorful marigolds can repel nematodes from the kitchen garden.

Companion Planting

Certain plants have a natural ability to repel specific pests and diseases. Make the most of these properties by pairing the plants that repel with the plants they protect. These associations include:

Geraniums repel Japanese beetles.

Marigolds repel nematodes and protect against bindweed and ground ivy invasions.

Garlic repels many insects and protects cabbage and cauliflower from aphids.

Dill guards cabbages against cabbage loopers.

Zinnia repels cucumber beetle and tomato worm.

Tomatoes repel asparagus beetles.

Sage protects against carrot rust flies.

Chives protect roses against blackspot, mildew, and pests.

Thyme protects against cabbageworm, snails, and slugs.

Parsley protects roses from rose beetles.

Black plastic warms soil for earlier spring planting.

n o matter where they live, it seems that gardeners bemoan the shortness of the

extending *the garden season*

growing season. But with a bit of effort, they can extend the growing season by days, weeks, or months.

The basic principle is to warm the air or the soil around the plants so they can grow.

Plastic Mulch

i t's a well-known fact that the color black absorbs sunlight. If you lay sheets of black plastic over the soil or on raised beds in late winter or early spring, the plastic will absorb the sun's warmth and warm the soil. This can add several weeks to the

gardening season. The plastic sheeting also keeps the soil from getting soggy from early spring rains and prevents weeds from growing.

Plants like melons and squash thrive in warm soil and appreciate the warming effects of the plastic well into the gardening season. Plant seedlings through the plastic by cutting slits or openings in the plastic— push the plastic aside to plant the seedlings. Bury the edges of the plastic or use rocks to keep it in place.

Cloches, Hotcaps, and Walls o' Water

O ver the years, gardeners have experimented with many

types of mini-green houses to warm a single plant. The idea is to bring the protection of a greenhouse to a plant that's grown in an outside environment.

A cloche is a small (6 to 18 inches high) glass, bottomless container that is shaped like a bell. It is placed over a plant to protect it from frost. Antique glass cloches are highly collectible and are now used more as ornaments. New cloches are in the marketplace.

Hotcaps are funnel-shaped "caps" that serve the same purpose as

cloches. You can make ones out of waxed paper, or buy clear or green-striped plastic ones. Unlike a cloche, they are unbreakable, and the top is open, so plants don't fry on a clear sunny day. Plastic milk jugs or two-liter bottles with the bottoms removed can also be used as hotcaps.

A recent development is the Wall o' Water. It holds water in a series of vertical plastic tubes connected into a ring, acting as a solar collector, absorbing the sun's warmth during the day and releasing it at night. It protects plants against freezing temperatures as low as 16 degrees F.

Cold Frames

a cold frame is a bottomless box with a clear plastic or glass lid. It can be quite simple, commercially made, or elaborately constructed. A simple cold frame consists of a pit dug in the corner of the garden covered by a discarded window sash.

Most gardeners find that a cold frame becomes an essential tool and as useful as a small greenhouse. In mild climates, use the cold frame to protect small crops from cold or frost. In some years and locations, crops can be grown in a cold frame through the winter.

In colder areas, the cold frame helps plants get an early start. They can be garden-ready several weeks early. You

Place Walls o' Water on the soil two weeks before planting to warm the soil.

can seed directly into a planting bed in the cold frame or use it for hardening off seedlings grown in the house.

Place the cold frame facing south or southwest. The back will usually be about six inches higher than the front. This will trap the heat inside and allow water to run off. You can gain additional heat by using microclimates in your garden. If you place it near a wall of a building, heat will be reflected, and that additional heat will be absorbed in the cold frame. A cold frame sunken 8 to 12 inches into the ground will retain heat even better.

Your cold frame lid can be made of a frame with plastic sheeting attached. Discarded window sashes are inexpensive and readily available but are heavy.

Build your cold frame out of rot-resistant wood.

Heat buildup during the day is a major consideration with cold frames. As the interior heat builds, you will have to vent the air to the outside. Whenever the interior temperature reaches 85° F, you need to let some heat out. This will occur on virtually all days except the coldest or very cloudy days. Prop the sash open with a stick. An alternative is an automatic opener that is solar powered. Check the amount of weight each will lift before building your cold frame.

In hot weather, some shading will help to prevent heat buildup. Use a lathe cover or shade cloth, or whitewash the glass. In very cold weather, you can help keep the heat in your cold frame by covering it with old blankets, carpet, or clean (seed-free) straw.

Hotbeds are cold frames with a built-in heating device. Electric heating cables are designed for just this purpose. Lay the cables on a base of sand. Cover them completely with sand, then lay wire mesh. Cover the mesh with an additional inch of sand. The bottom heat from the cable encourages seedlings and other plants to grow rapidly. It keeps them growing in colder weather than they could normally withstand.

Row Covers and Tunnels

There are two basic types of row covers. The floating row cover is a lightweight synthetic fabric that rests directly on your plants. Hoops or frames support the heavier plastic types, forming a tunnel over plants. The floating covers are easy to use and allow light and some water to penetrate. They can remain on during the season and help prevent damage from flying insects. The plastic row covers have a lower initial cost but require more labor to install because of the frames needed. Minimize the labor by pounding 10-inch sections of galvanized or PVC pipe into the ground at each corner and at about 3-foot intervals around the beds or inside edges of raised beds. Leave a few inches of pipe exposed above ground. The inside diameter of the pipe should be large enough to accommodate the PVC pipe used for hoops.

Bend the pipe to create the structure for the tunnel. Use the pipe holder to hold plant supports later in the season. Also, use the hoops to support blanket covers late in the season.

Curved cold frame covers allow taller plants to keep growing in autumn.

Choice of Materials

Some vining plants, such as tomatoes, cucumbers, climbing roses, pole beans, and peas, need a structure or support to grow on. Structures keep vegetables and fruit off the ground, prevent damage, and improve

Wood and other natural materials are often preferred for their natural look in a kitchen garden. On the other hand, plastic and rust-resistant metals will last longer and require little maintenance. Copper pipe, for example, assumes a wonderful greenish patina after outdoor exposure.

Quick and simple

support, or leaned against a building. Plants will happily clamber up all of them.

When building a structure, choose wood that lasts well without paint and will weather

From Stakes to the Tepee

the simplest support a gardener can use is a single stake. Stakes are available in many sizes, colors, and

bittersweet, grape vine, jute, or lightweight rope. To set in place, push the legs of the tepee into the ground. Tepees are easy to move or store in the fall. Use small tepees in containers, larger ones in the garden.

Trellises

a simple trellis is a framed structure with cross pieces, standing upright or at an angle to support climbing plants. Woven wire fencing, netting, wood, or twine can be attached to a frame constructed of wood or pipe (metal or PVC). Combine two into an A-frame by attaching them together at the top with hinges. This structure is portable, adjustable, and will support plants on two different sides.

Construct a bean harp from a wood or pipe

gardens need a support system

the appearance of the garden. Structures help you make the best use of vertical space by allowing you to grow more in the same area.

supports can be adapted from found objects. Old ladders and head and footboards from beds can be used directly in the garden, with some

naturally. Cedar, redwood, and others blend into, rather than stand out in, the garden. Select from what is available locally. Use brass or galvanized screws, nails, hardware, and other connectors for the longest lasting construction.

materials. You can also use trimmings from shrubs and trees that blend well with the garden.

Combine three or more stakes and tie them together near the top to make a tepee. You can build a tepee out of bamboo stakes, concrete reinforcing rods (rebar), copper pipe, tree saplings, 2×2s, or other materials. Bind them together at the top with willow wands,

frame, with twine sections attached to the top and bottom piece. Beans or other plants can grow up the twine. When frost hits and kills the plants, cut the twine and vines and put all of it into the compost pile.

You can make a multi-sectioned screen from twigs or willow. Like a room-dividing screen, you can move this outdoor structure where needed as a plant support, or to create a visual screen or division.

A trellis can be permanently installed or can be used in different locations throughout the years. Use pipe with a slightly larger inside diameter than the trellis legs for a stronger installation. Pound sections of the pipe into the ground in spots where the trellis legs will be. Use pipe sections attached to the sides of raised beds for readily available support.

Design more elaborate structures to fulfill other needs or desires. A path can be decorated with matching upright trellises connected with an arch. This type has been typically used for roses but can also accommodate other vining plants.

Fences

a perimeter fence can mark the kitchen garden. The fence can keep out wildlife, act as a windbreak, be a decorative element on its own, or provide a place for plants to grow and climb upward. Consider what look you wish to achieve. A white picket fence, for instance, suggests a colonial garden that would be formal and neat. A woven fence, or wattle, could enclose an herb garden. A twig fence or split rail fence suggests a relaxed or rustic feeling.

Building a Stick Fence

t o construct a stick fence, first look closely at a simple picket fence. Notice that rails attach to the outside of the posts, then the pickets to the outside of rails. Observe the balanced placement of all the components.

If possible, use locust posts; untreated and sunk directly in the soil, they will resist rot for years.

For a stick fence, set other types of posts in individual concrete footings or treat with wood preservative. Use pine 1×4s as rails, treating them first for moisture resistance.

Using staple nails and wire, attach a strip of hardware cloth from the lower rail down to the ground as a rabbit deterrent. Always use green wood for the stick pickets, as old wood is difficult to work with.

Ash is good—after a few months the bark falls away and it weathers to a lovely gray. Attach the sticks using galvanized finishing nails, driving them in at an angle. Position the sticks about four feet apart, allowing them to extend completely to the ground. Leave them a bit tall at first, then use a sharp pair of loppers to fashion your own pattern along the top of the fence. Build the gate last, hinging and bracing it.

Attaching Plants

S imply guide lightweight vines with tendrils onto support structures. Attach others with soft material; do not use wire or ties with wire in the centers. The metal will harm soft tissue. Support heavy fruit like melons. Wood trellises can be designed to accommodate small, movable shelves.

Birdhouses

A piece of an old fence is the elegant end to a bed. Later it will support pea vines.

a kitchen garden differs aesthetically from a basic vegetable garden: A vegetable garden is utilitarian, while a kitchen garden begs to be decorated.

Plants can be a sculptured element and become a focal point in the garden. An old, gnarled, lichen-covered fruit tree has charm and style. A gardener can shape shrubs and trees.

b irds have long been important to gardeners—they help keep insect pests in control. In Tudor times, the columbarium, or pigeon house, was a feature in most of the great gardens of Europe. The Chinese-influenced dovecotes became popular in eighteenth century England.

Today birdhouses are available in a wide variety of styles: dovecotes, purple martin houses, carved gourds,

Water in the Garden

h istorically, kitchen gardens had a well or running water at their centers. Today, a commonplace hose or sprinkler delivers most water needs. Consider adding

shops. There are many novel sprinkler designs, including flower shapes.

A birdbath is both practical and visually interesting. A large rock

Scarecrows

S carecrows are mostly for fun—they probably won't keep the birds away from your berries (use netting). Simply enjoy the design process and your end result. Commercially made forms are now available, or you can make your own with sticks, straw, wire, and your imagination. You can even have someone's face printed on cloth. Dress the scarecrow like your friend or any way you desire. Accessorize with hats, scarves, gloves, and more. If you use work gloves, they will always be handy for weeding.

a bit of ornament for fun

Topiary, espaliered plants on a wall, or a formal hedge set a tone. A dancing bear, lyre-shaped apple tree, or manicured boxwood hedge reflect different style choices. One gardener even shaped a creeping fig into the shape of his favorite state—Texas.

log cabins, and even miniature replicas of your own house. Many birdhouses are collectible.

a decorative faucet shaped like a bird or other interesting shape, or search for old sprinklers in antiques

or stone with a depression in the top is a natural bath. A shallow pool or water garden is another possibility. Birds and frogs will have no problem finding either.

This scarecrow might not frighten the birds, but she decorates the garden well.

Sculpture

Sculpture is the true art in a kitchen garden. It can be large or small, modern or classic, kinetic or static. Whatever it is, it attracts interest. Use sculpture as a focal point at the center or corners of the garden.

One gardener has a beautiful marble nude in her garden made by the court sculptor of Czar Nicholas. She enjoys it, but such art is out of reach for most gardeners.

Gardening design tastes for others run more to large chain saw-carved wooden animals and birds. If you are creative, you can make your own sculpture. One gardener liked making wooden animals and carved a whole series of birds and attached them to fence posts.

If your taste is a bit more classical, there are reasonably priced quality reproductions—from saints (St. Fiacre is the patron saint of gardens, not St. Francis), to gargoyles, to animals of all sorts—available in weatherproof materials.

Found Art

Garage sales, antique shops, or even the dump or junkyard can yield ornamental treasures. Several manmade objects can be adapted for garden use. Metal fragments and architectural remnants are dramatic when placed well. Wood posts, finials, auto parts, stone sinks, metal fencing, and gates are treasures.

Be bold in your choices and in preparing the pieces for use. Clean

A sundial surrounded by lavender marks the center of the garden.

or paint them in whatever colors excite you.

One gardener hangs old tools on a garden shed for interest. She accents beds with pleasing shapes of driftwood and weathered wood. Another gardener currently ornaments his garden with several old cultivators, a wooden wheelbarrow, and a weather vane. Some gardeners are more

An old watering can is part of a kinetic sculpture that keeps water plants happy.

flamboyant in their tastes—pink flamingos are popping up everywhere.

Start looking at gardens—you'll see old metal work turned into gates, helix-shaped blades from reel lawn mowers transformed into sculptures, and hitching posts that accent herb gardens. Does this give you ideas? It's your garden. Just have fun!

Seating and Eating

Create casual seating by cutting a large log in half lengthwise. Make a bench by supporting the split log with smaller log sections. A slab of granite supported by chunks of granite also makes a solid and naturalistic bench. Artisans shape chairs from large tree trunks and construct tables from similar trees with wood slab tops. These rustic sets look like something out of Alice in Wonderland.

Twig furniture gives a lighter yet rustic appearance. Impromptu seating can be fashioned by wrapping neatly cut bundles of firewood with a piece of strong wire. New commercially produced metal chairs have floral and foliage pattern motifs that work well in the garden. Search for Victorian cast-iron sets or other antique garden furniture in antiques shops. Adapt an old metal sewing machine base to hold a glass top to serve as a small table. And who can resist the simple tire swing or a hammock hung between two trees?

A harvest of herbs, ready to go into the kitchen, is beautiful as a bouquet.

herbs are now grown for somewhat different reasons than they were historically. The ancients used herbs as their pharmacopoeia. Herbs were their only drugs.

The monasteries of Europe always had a physic garden to provide medicines, along with condiments, for the monks. Much lore, legend, and superstition are part

of the tradition of growing and using herbs.

Today, herbs are appreciated for their beauty and happily coexist with showy annual and perennial flowers. Cooks know the value of fresh herbs to liven the most mundane of dishes.

Some gardeners grow herbs for use in craft projects—dried wreaths, nosegays, and potpourri. Many herbs are still used as dye plants to color cloth.

A tea garden can produce enough leaves for many cups of tea and afternoons of tea parties.

What is an Herb?

botanists define an herb as a plant that does not have persistent woody above ground parts—a plant that dies back to the ground in winter.

an herbal garden of delights

Most gardeners think of herbs as useful plants—plants used for food, flavoring, fragrance, beverages, medicine, perfume, crafts, or dyeing.

Herbs can be annual, perennial, shrub, or tree. The word is pronounced "herb" and "erb," depending on where you live. Both are right—call them whatever you want; they are plants we couldn't live without.

Combine annual flowers and herbs for lovely plantings.

Growing Herbs

Cultural needs vary from plant to plant, but most herbs prefer full sun and well-drained soil. Many culinary herbs develop the most intense flavor and more volatile oil if grown in lean, not-too-rich soils. Many herbs will survive in rich, organic soil—they'll grow lushly, but will be less useful for fragrance and flavoring.

Add little or no fertilizer to the herb garden. The herbs listed opposite for growing in the shade will tolerate

soils that are more organic. The silver and gray-leafed plants are the most sensitive. Most are native to the Mediterranean countries and need good drainage and full sun.

Growing Herbs in the South

hot and humid climates challenge the herb gardener. A few things will help improve your chances of success. The single most important route to success is

providing soil that drains very quickly.

Raised beds create the proper drainage for herbs, but so can carefully placing herbs in the garden. Normally, plants are put in the soil at the same level they were growing in the pot. For best drainage, plant herbs high, even in the top of a little mound of well-drained soil added on top of the planting bed. Use gravel mulch around herbs. Place herbs in a location with adequate air circulation.

Using all, or part, of these techniques will require you to water more frequently in hot weather, which proves the techniques are beneficial. In the warmest areas, grow herbs during cool winter months. Plant seeds of basil, borage, marjoram, and thyme in September for harvest throughout the season.

Herbs in the Kitchen Garden

Many gardeners don't have room for a formal herb garden. Herbs can be combined with vegetables or in a mixed flower border. Parsley and basil make attractive edging plants.

Interplant delicate plants of dill, chervil, and fennel almost anywhere. They will act as fillers in borders—much as baby's-breath does in bouquets. They're also great in fresh arrangements.

Silver and variegated sages look good, in flower or not, in the flower border. Chives produce a lush flower display several times a season if cut back after flowering. Plant herbs with fragrant leaves near paths. Brushing them as you walk by will release their fragrance. Use pineapple sage, chocolate mint, verbena, and thymes this way.

herbs

herbs for the shade

These herbs will tolerate some degree of shade (most herbs perform better in full sun):

- Angelica
- Anise hyssop
- Basil
- Bloodroot
- Chervil
- Chives
- Coltsfoot
- Costmary
- Lemon balm
- Lovage
- Mint
- Parsley
- Saffron crocus
- Sweet cicely
- Sweet woodruff
- Tarragon

herbs used in cooking

(Leaves used for all; other parts used are indicated)

- Basil (flowers)
- Bay
- Borage (flowers)
- Chives (flowers)
- Cilantro (flowers; seeds are called coriander)
- Dill (flowers, seeds)
- Mint
- Oregano
- Parsley (stems)
- Rosemary (flowers)
- Tarragon
- Thyme (flowers)

silver and gray-leaved herbs

- Artemisia
- Basil, camphor
- Betony, woolly
- Chamomile
- Dittany of Crete
- Lamb's-ears
- Lamium
- Lavender
- Lemon balm
- Mint, apple
- Rue
- Sage
- Southernwood
- Wormwood

herbs for tea

- Angelica
- Anise hyssop
- Cicely
- Lemon verbena
- Mint
- Rosemary
- Sage

native american herbs

- Black birch
- Bloodroot
- Butterfly weed
- Cardinal flower
- Dog-tooth violet
- Jack-in-the-pulpit
- Jerusalem artichoke
- Meadow rue
- New Jersey tea
- Sassafras
- Trillium
- Wild ginger

Vine-ripened tomatoes make mouths water.

When Texas singer-songwriter Guy Clark introduces his song "Homegrown Tomatoes" he says he's about to sing a love song. America loves homegrown tomatoes. They are the most important vegetable grown in the home garden.

America were the first to cultivate them, as ornamentals. The Aztecs were the first to cultivate and eat them; giving them the name tomato (*tomatl* or *xtomatl*). This was a wild form of the cherry tomato (*Lycopersicon esculentum* var. *cerasiforme*), from which modern tomatoes are descended.

In about 1520, Cortez found tomatoes in an Aztec market and took the seed to Spain. In 1522, they were introduced to Italy, then

tomato as a curiosity and as an ornamental plant. The French called them *pomme d'amour*, the love apple, while the Italians named them *pomo d'oro*, the golden apple, suggesting that a yellow variety was known.

Early botanists placed the tomato in the nightshade family, which

colonists, brought plants or seed back from Europe to the New World. The tomato remained mostly an ornamental plant until the 1800s.

By 1835, tomatoes were widely available and were

growing gorgeous tomatoes

History

Tomatoes are native to the Andes Mountains of South America. The pre-Mayans in Central

under Spanish rule. The Italians were the first Europeans to both cultivate and eat the tomato. The balance of Europe treated the

includes many poisonous plants. The stems and leaves of plants in this family are toxic and have occasionally killed imprudently grazing livestock.

Thomas Jefferson was among the first Americans to cultivate tomatoes, raising them at Monticello in 1781. He, like many

used in catsup, preserves, and pickles. Still, suspicion lingered, and cookbooks warned cooks to cook tomatoes for over three hours to remove the raw taste.

In 1880, six distinct types were offered in one catalog. W. Atlee Burpee listed 22 varieties in its 1888 Farm Annual catalog including 'Golden Queen', describing it as "handsome yellow slices making a beautiful contrast in dishes with the red tomatoes."

Growth Habit

Tomatoes have three different types of growth habit. Determinate tomatoes are generally small plants. They grow bush-like and stop growing when fruit is set. The semideterminate varieties grow to a bit larger size. Both types flower and set fruit within a short time span, producing a short harvest season. Some varieties have picking seasons of only a week to 10 days.

Indeterminate tomatoes really are vines and will continue to grow and bear fruit until killed by frost or disease. These require staking for best performance.

'Green Zebra' produces delicious, emerald green, sweet-tart fruit.

The Kindest Pinch

there has been much debate about pinching tomatoes to control the number of fruit-producing stems.

A single-stem plant will usually yield the earliest fruit, but not as much fruit as a multi-stem plant. Two or more stems will produce more fruit. The additional foliage of a multi-stemmed plant will help to protect the tomatoes from the sun. If multiple stems are allowed to develop, the plant will need to be supported.

It is best to pinch any unwanted growing shoot after it has developed two leaves. By pinching out the growing point above those leaves, the fruit will be bigger.

Size

an incredible variety of shapes, colors, and sizes of tomatoes are available to grow from seed. The Tomato Growers Supply Company lists more than 300 tomato varieties, including 100 heirlooms.

Cherry tomatoes are the smallest, weighing from about an ounce. The fruit is produced in grape-like clusters. Harvest them regularly to avoid cracking. 'Sweet 100', 'Gardener's Delight', and 'Small Fry' all produce 1-inch, red fruit. 'Tiny Tim' is a bit smaller, and 'Micro-Tom' is the smallest—the plant is only 5 to 8 inches tall with tasty fruit smaller than a marble. 'Tiny Tim', 'Micro-Tom', and 'Small Fry' are good for containers.

Plum- and pear-shaped fruit weigh between 2 and 6 ounces. They are very meaty and have thick walls and less gel than other tomatoes—good for making sauce. 'Roma' and 'Chico III' produce 3- to 4-ounce fruits.

Medium tomatoes weigh from 6 to 16 ounces. Well-known examples are 'Better Boy' and 'Early Girl', both good for slicing.

The big bruisers are the beefsteaks. They are meaty, firm, and big. They can produce giant fruits weighing up to 2 pounds.

Color

in a recent analysis of seed catalogs by the Seed Savers Exchange, they found that there were 82 orange to yellow, 65 pink to purple, 434 red, and 62 other colored tomato varieties listed for sale. Tomatoes range from creamy white through lime green to pink, yellow, golden, orange, and red.

A very unusual Russian heirloom is 'Silvery Fir Tree', which has delicate, lacy, fuzzy leaves with a silvery sheen.

Nonred tomatoes tend to be milder-flavored. Yellow and orange ones aren't lower in acid content than the reds— they're milder in flavor.

The unusual-hued tomatoes make colorful

All of the tomato varieties pictured here are ripe and ready to eat.

additions to the table and the landscape. Black and purple types include the richly flavored 'Black Krim', with a hint of saltiness. The truest purple color is found in 'Purple Calabash', which is distinguished by its rich and winey flavor and unusual fluted, almost ruffled, shape. White and ivory fruit is produced by 'White Wonder', 'White Beauty', and 'Snow White'.

Yellow 'Banana Legs' is great for making tomato paste, 'Brandywine' (yellow) is a big slicing type, and 'Lemon Boy' is the first true lemon-yellow hybrid. There are also many striped, bicolor, and orange varieties.

Imagine mixing these small fruits together in a salad: 'Yellow Pear'— 1 ounce yellow pear-shape; 'Green Grape'— 1-inch green with yellow highlights; 'Super Sweet 100'—extra-sweet red cherry; and 'Red Currant'—currant-sized, rich-flavored fruit.

Tomatoes planted in insulated towers get off to an early start—ready to eat by July 4.

Taste

Taste in tomatoes, like everything else in life, is highly personal. A recent taste test at Quail Hill farm cooperative on Long Island ranked the cherry tomato 'Sungold' No. 1 with its optimal sweetness. Other winners, listed in ranking from the best included: 'Matt's Wild Cherry' (tiny, sweet, red), 'Glacier' (red standard), 'Brandywine' (pink with red flesh), 'Persimmon' (orange standard), 'Firebird' (red standard), 'Tommy Toes' (apricot-sized cherry), 'Moskvich' (red standard), 'Cherokee Purple' (purple standard, originally cultivated by the Cherokees).

At David Cavagnaro's farm in Iowa, another group of tasters picked their favorites. They ranked 'Amish Paste' the best. It's an acorn-shaped variety intended for making paste, yet was wonderful for salads and voted the best, multiple-use tomato. Other top-ranked varieties follow: 'Tommy Toes' (also called 'Steakhouse') (heirloom red), 'Brandywine' (the yellow one, this time), 'Sungold', 'Super Sweet 100' (cherry red, tall-growing, heavy yield), 'Una's Yellow Cherry' (yellow cherry), 'Una's Ruby Cluster' (large, red cherry), and 'Green Zebra' (gold striped).

In Northern California taste-test winners include: 'Early Girl', 'Golden Mandarin Cross', 'Better Boy', 'Golden Jubilee', 'Yellow Pear', 'Striped Cavern', 'White Beauty', and 'Red Currant'.

Maturity—Time to Harvest

Tomatoes are also classified according to the length of time from transplanting to harvest. This is the time span from planting a healthy seedling outdoors until harvest of the first fruit.

Early tomatoes take from 55 to 65 days to ripen. Midseason is about 66 to 80 days, while anything requiring over 80 days to ripen is considered a late variety.

It's not surprising that many of the fast-maturing tomatoes have descriptive names: 'Early Girl' (52 days), 'Early Cascade' (55 days), 'Bush Early Girl' (54 days), or 'Early Swedish' (65 days). Others suggest their origins in the cold, short-growing season parts of the world: 'Polar Beauty' (63 days), 'Polar Star' (65 days), 'Siberia' (55 days), and 'Sub Arctic Maxi' (62 days).

Midseason tomatoes include the popular hybrids 'Big Boy' (78 days), 'Better Boy' (75 days), and 'Big Girl' (78 days).

Good varieties for the south include 'Gulf State Market' (78 days) and 'Hawaiian' (70 days), a heat-resistant plant that produces smooth, large, 10-ounce fruits.

Long-season types include 'Wonder Boy' (80 days) and 'Super Bush' (85 days).

Get Started Early

Garden bragging rights usually go to the first local tomato of the season, especially in cold climates. This can be a challenge, as the tomato's preferred growing temperature range is a rather narrow 55 to 85 degrees F.

Start by sowing your seed exactly eight weeks prior to when night and day temperatures are above 55 degrees F. Germinate the seed at 75 to 80 degrees F. Ideal growing conditions mimic nature, with night temperatures dropping to 55 degrees F for about

Tomatoes, mulched with straw to prevent weeds, will soon grow as tall as their cages.

three weeks, then at 65 to 70 degrees F. Give them at least eight hours of sun per day—more would be better.

The seedlings can also be grown under fluorescent lights. Keep the growing tips within a few inches of the lights for 16 hours per day. Research has shown that gently shaking the seedling containers or allowing air to move the seedlings produces stronger-growing plants.

When the plants begin to touch, move them to larger containers. Slowly harden off the seedlings by moving them to partly shaded outdoor locations over a period of a few days. Then move them into full sun.

Plant them in prepared soil that has been moistened with a mild solution of fertilizer. Always plant them with the first set of true leaves at ground level. If the seedlings have etiolated (stretched out), lay them sideways in a shallow trench and cover all but the top set of leaves. They will root all along the stem and produce a much stronger plant.

For the earliest fruit, try some of these tricks: Warm the ground by covering it a few weeks before planting with black plastic mulch. Use a collar of black plastic mulch around each plant; leave room to water. Red plastic mulch has been shown to improve tomato yields and may produce earlier fruit. Keep your plants warm at night by covering with blankets over a wire cage, cloches, Walls o' Water, hotcaps, rose cones, plastic jugs with the bottoms removed, water-filled black inner tubes, or other methods of retaining heat. Use cold frames, plastic film tunnels, arched fiberglass panels, and minigreenhouses in much the same way. Some growers have even used a heating cable (insulated, seed-starting type) buried below the root system. Pinch plants to a single stem for earliest fruit.

Disease Resistance

One good way to deal with diseases of tomatoes is to grow varieties that are genetically resistant. Verticillium wilt and fusarium wilt are diseases that can destroy your crop and for which there is no effective treatment. Nematodes are tiny microscopic pests that eat, weaken, and destroy plant roots. Seed packets or catalogs will indicate that varieties are resistant to these problems with the labels: "V" for verticillium wilt, "F" for fusarium wilt, and "N" for nematodes. A few catalogs also label those plants resistant to tobacco mosaic virus with a "T" and alternaria with an "A."

Tomatillos and Ground Cherries

The tomatillo (*Physalis ixocarpa*) and ground cherry (*Physalis pubescens*) are not true tomatoes but are usually listed near them in seed catalogs. They are annuals, growing to 3 to 4 feet in height, producing tart-tasting or sweet fruit. Use the sweet fruit of the ground cherry in any way you would use other fruit.

The tomatillo is used in Mexican food. The distinctive tart flavor (raw or cooked) is the "secret" to phenomenal salsas, salads, tacos, and sandwiches. Grow just like tomatoes. Store in a cool place with the fruit left on the vine and in their husks. They will keep for months. Tomatillo varieties 'Toma Verde' and 'Verde Puebla' have small green fruit inside a tan, papery husk that you remove before use. A more decorative and sweeter fruit is the 'Purple de Milpa' variety.

Tomatillos are easy to grow in the garden and make a great addition to salsas.

'Medallion' is a handsome, deep green Romaine lettuce.

The leafy salad vegetables, especially lettuces, are popular with gardeners and cooks. Most are easy to grow and produce an edible crop quickly. They produce large returns in a small area. Most are ready to pick in a short time, as few as 45 days.

Greens add texture to a salad or a meal, often with a nice crunch. Flavors vary from subtle and mild to bitter, lemony, or strong. Some will stand alone; blend others to create the balance you desire. Their appearance on the plate as well as in the garden creates many an opportunity for personal expression, from diminutive leaves to giant, in-your-face ones. Some are flat; others are crinkly or savoyed. Thin and delicate leaf texture contrasts with big, bold, stature.

A plethora of solid green shades only begins the leafy vegetable color range. There are green leaves edged with red. Others are red, purple, gray, silver, or maroon, along with multicolors, and even freckles. They are wonderful foliage plants for the garden, decorative on a plate, taste treats for the palate, and fun and easy to grow.

History

Lettuce has supplied the leafy soul of the salad throughout the world for centuries. Virgil's poem "The Salad" is over 2,000 years old. Even the word "salad" is derived from the practice of dipping greens into salt. Persian kings treated their guests to lettuce. The Egyptians and Assyrians considered lettuce an aphrodisiac.

Historians have found Egyptian tomb drawings of upright-growing lettuce with long leaves that seem to be about 3 to 6 inches wide. Pliny described nine varieties that the Romans grew during classical times. They had found one type of upright lettuce growing on the island of Kos (or Cos). It was so popular in Rome that eventually the name was changed to *romaine*.

By the late fourteenth century, the English were using greens, including lettuce, mixed with herbs, onions, and leeks "mingled" with oil, vinegar, and salt. By Elizabethan times, lettuce was combined with other greens: chicory, cress, dandelion, mustard, spinach, purslane, sorrel, radish, and turnip greens.

Over the years, lettuces went in and out of favor. For a while, iceberg types dominated, but today a wide variety of lettuces are among the many greens served in salads.

Types

There are four basic types (and one intermediate type) of lettuce: looseleaf lettuce, crisphead lettuce, butterhead lettuce, romaine lettuce, and batavian.

LOOSELEAF LETTUCE Looseleaf lettuce, also known as leaf lettuce (*Lactuca sativa* var. *crispa*), forms a loose, nonheading rosette of curled or fringed leaves. It is the earliest of all the lettuces and matures in 40–45 days.

Looseleaf lettuce is the easiest and most adaptable lettuce for the home gardener. The range of taste, color, and texture affords choices

A collection of heirloom lettuces shows their varied form and color.

the king of salad greens—lettuce

'Red sails' brightens the garden and the salad bowl with its rich coloring.

for everyone. A few square feet of space can produce a small crop. Select one of the cut-and-come-again varieties: leaves snipped for a salad will soon be replaced with new growth.

Green-leafed Varieties
'Black-Seeded Simpson' is an old favorite dating back to about 1850. It's a very popular, early spring variety with light green, tasty leaves.

'Green Ice' has blistered, savoyed, glossy dark green leaves with fringed edges. It is very slow to go to seed and is widely available.

'Royal Oakleaf' has a more definitive oakleaf shape than 'Oakleaf'. It produces large, medium to deep green rosettes that stand well in the garden.

'Salad Bowl' is a fast-maturing (only 40 days), popular, All-America Selections Winner. It's very easy to grow and heat-resistant. The large, long, frilly, lime green leaves look

great in a salad. Although it looks like one, it is not a true oakleaf lettuce.

Red-Leafed Varieties
'Merlot' is an intense, burgundy-colored lettuce that stands out in a mixed salad or planting. It is slow to bolt and works well for cut-and-come-again culture.

'Red Sails' is a very popular, All-American Selections Winner. It is fast maturing (only 45 days) with crinkled, maroon red leaves. The red hue intensifies as the leaves mature. It is heat-tolerant, slow to bolt and, best of all, very slow to turn bitter.

Baby Leaf Lettuce
'Biondo Lisce' is a small-leafed, tender Italian lettuce that should be cut several times when young. Start cutting the light green leaves about one month after planting. New leaves grow vigorously to replace the ones just cut. You must cut it in warm months or it will bolt.

CRISPHEAD LETTUCE
The crisphead lettuce (*Lactuca sativa* var. *capitata*) forms a distinct, cabbage-like head and is a textural standout with very crisp leaves. It is harder and more durable in storage and handling, notwithstanding the thinner leaves. The familiar iceberg type available in every supermarket exemplifies this group. It produces big, solid heads of tightly packed leaves. It

has lots of crunch and mouth-feel but little flavor and little food value. It supplies less vitamin A and C than other varieties.

This type of lettuce has been well known since the sixteenth century when it was first recognized as a distinct type. Crispheads are the slowest to mature (70 to 90 days) and the most demanding of rich soil and cool temperatures. They need lots of phosphorus in order to form solid heads. Most gardeners should choose other, more forgiving types of lettuce.

Crisphead Varieties
'Ithaca' ('Improved Iceberg') is a form of iceberg. It was bred for tough conditions and produces a nice, medium, dark green

head with good flavor.

'Rosy' ('Rosa') is one of the easiest crispheads to grow. It is quite heat-tolerant and produces sweet, crunchy, and juicy heads under tough conditions. A taste-test winner, it has deep burgundy outer leaves surrounding a medium, green head.

'Summertime' was developed to perform well at the higher temperatures of the Northwest throughout the summer. Swirled, fringed leaves form compact heads about 6 inches wide by 5 inches deep.

BUTTERHEAD LETTUCE
Butterhead lettuce is more fragile in texture than the crisphead types. The thicker leaves have a smooth and buttery substance. The leaves form an open, rather soft head of pale heart leaves surrounded by darker outer leaves. This is considered the first American gourmet lettuce. Most varieties are ready in 50–75 days.

Butterhead Varieties
'Bibb' is both the type (the term "butterhead" was formed to describe 'Bibb') and a specific variety that was bred in Kentucky in the 1850s by Jack Bibb. Delicate and deliciously flavored, soft green leaves cup to form a soft head.

'Buttercrunch' is an All-America Selections Winner. It is heat-tolerant and has good bolt resistance. It is a reliable performer with a compact head of dark green leaves.

'Four Seasons' ('Merveille des Quatre Saisons') is a beautifully colored and textured lettuce. It features crisp burgundy outer leaves and softer-textured cream and pink center ones.

'Mescher' is an Austrian family heirloom from the 1700s that was brought to the United States after 1900. It forms a nice crisp, tight head of green leaves ringed with red. It has a wonderful taste and appearance. It is best grown in cool weather and is very cold-hardy.

'Tom Thumb' is a cute, baby lettuce with apple-sized, medium green, crumpled heads. Serve it whole as an individual salad. It's fun to grow in pots or containers.

ROMAINE LETTUCE
Romaine or Cos lettuce (*Lactuca sativa* var. *longifolia*) has long, oval, overlapping leaves that stand erect. An older name for romaine is celery lettuce because of the similarly shaped growth habit. The outer leaves are smooth, covering the blanched inner leaves. All have a strong midrib. The significant leaf substance can stand the rough tossing required of it when incorporating it in a Caesar salad. The nice, big-sized leaf makes it convenient for a sandwich.

Romaine Varieties
'Deer Tongue' ('Matchless', 'Rodin') is an heirloom that received its name from its uniquely triangular-shaped, round-tipped leaves. Leaves look a bit like spinach and are somewhat savoyed with a succulent midrib. Its very good, sweet, buttery flavor and crisp texture make it worth a little extra effort (it's not very heat-tolerant). It can form a head, but most gardeners use it as a cut-and-come-again lettuce.

'Freckles' ('Trout Back') is an exquisite-looking lettuce. Lime green, oblong leaves are freckled with wine red markings. Cut leaves at 4–6 inches for tender texture.

'Rouge d'Hiver' ('Red River') has deep red leaves that form a loose, romaine head. It is a cold- and heat-tolerant romaine with good flavor. Cool temperatures and high light produce the best leaf color.

BATAVIAN LETTUCE
Batavian lettuce is a European-developed semiheading form of crisphead lettuce. It is softer in leaf texture, making it virtually impossible to ship and a perfect treat for the home gardener to grow and eat. Young plants consist of individual leaves, which later develop into a loosely wrapped small head at maturity. The leaves are mild and

somewhat sweet-tasting, yet crisp. It sometimes is called French crisp lettuce. It takes about 50 days to mature.

Batavian Varieties
'Anuenue' (pronounced ah-new-ee-new-ee) was bred at the University of Hawaii for heat resistance. It looks like a small iceberg-type lettuce but is much easier to grow, is more heat-resistant, and has a mild and juicy taste.

'Red Grenoble' ('Roter Grenobler' or 'Rouge Grenobloise') is a vigorous and reliable performer. Shiny, wine red, curly leaves can be cut young or allowed to form a tight central head. Plant in spring or fall, as it's not as heat-resistant as some varieties.

'Reine des Glaces' ('Ice Queen') is a gorgeous lettuce with deeply incised or notched leaves that form a convoluted, somewhat hollow, frosted green head. It's juicy, crisp with a touch of nutty flavor, and good for spring planting.

Cultivating Lettuce

Most varieties prefer a light, well-drained, organic soil that retains moisture. A slightly acidic soil (pH 5.5–6.5) is best. All lettuces need a constant supply of moisture throughout the growing cycle. Water in the morning to allow leaves to dry before evening. This will help prevent downy mildew.

Don't fertilize heavily, as research has shown that excess nitrogen makes lettuce bitter. The best nutritional source is from compost-rich, organic soil. Apply foliar fertilizer (fertilizer mixed with water and sprayed on the leaves) lightly until two weeks before harvest.

Lettuce prefers full sun locations except in the summer or in southern regions, when it will benefit from some shade. It is adaptable enough that you can produce crops in shady locations, if that is all that is available.

Lettuce is a cool-weather crop. Carefully select types and varieties that perform best in your region of the country and in the season you want to grow them. Romaine is the most adaptable to warm-weather conditions.

For the earliest crop, start lettuce seed indoors six to seven weeks before the last frost date. Plant seedlings even when frost is forecast. A light frost will not kill them. Continue sowing small amounts of seed every few weeks in the garden. Space seedlings or thin to about 6 inches apart for baby varieties, 8 inches for most others, and 12 to 15 inches apart for heading types.

In warm climates and in summer, you can shade lettuce with lathe to keep it cool.

Mesclun

Mesclun is not a specific type of lettuce but a mixture of lettuce and other leafy vegetables. Virtually every seed catalog lists several such mixtures. They may include several types of lettuce, arugula, cress, frisée, mâche, mizuna, purslane, and others that are detailed in the following pages.

Mesclun has become increasingly popular with gardeners and cooks—for good reason. It is a great way to experiment with new plants, flavors, and textures.

Mesclun allows you to sow a mix in an open spot in the garden without much thought or planning (just have the seed on hand). In a few weeks, that new crop is ready.

'Ruby' chard is elegant in the garden, growing here with Japanese red mustard.

The leafy vegetables detailed below are primarily used raw and for salads. Most are easy to grow and require no more effort than lettuce.

ARUGULA (*Eruca vesicaria* ssp. *sativa*)
Also known as rocket and roquette, it's a piquant, peppery Mediterranean green. Grow in cool weather and harvest young leaves to avoid the bitterness that develops in hot weather. Sow seed about one-half inch deep as early in the spring as the soil can be worked. Keep well-watered and harvest young.

CHICORY (*Cichorium intybus*)
Europeans have hybridized chicory into a diverse group of plants. Eat cutting chicories alone as an ethnic Italian treat or combine with part of a mesclun seeding. 'Ceriolo' has a texture like buttercrunch lettuce, while others, like 'Dentarella', are tart on the tongue. 'Catalogna' looks like, and is sometimes sold as, dandelion. Harvest it anytime, from baby size, in about three weeks, or wait until big, 18-inch-tall bunches develop.

Endive
Belgian endive or Witloof chicory is the classic blanched mesclun component. It is a type of chicory grown and harvested as a root crop after the first frost. Store the roots in moist sand at 35–40 degrees F. Force the roots to grow in complete darkness at about 55 degrees F and 95 percent humidity. Harvest when the chicons (sprouts) are 4 to 6 inches long. The yellow-white crispy leaves have a mild, bittersweet flavor.

Escarole
This chicory has wavy, broad outer leaves that are tough and best cooked. The blanched inner leaves look like the hearts of buttercrunch lettuce and add a nice touch to salad.

Frisée
This is a finely textured, almost lacy-leaf form of endive. Young leaves, both outer ones and the blanched inner leaves, are great for salad. 'Galia' and 'Tres Fine Maraicher' are fast producing (45 to 48 days) varieties.

Radicchio
This is the red, heading form of chicory. In zone 8, grow it through winter for early spring harvest. In colder areas, it needs to be forced. Plant in late May and cut it back after Labor Day. Harvest the new growth in about 4 to 6 weeks. 'Red Treviso' is a gorgeous variety with narrow, deep burgundy leaves and bright white midribs.

New nonforcing, 'Chiogga' radicchios are treated like winter-hardy lettuce. Plant in early spring and harvest 60 to 75 days later. 'Giulio' is an early variety (burgundy leaves with white ribs) that forms small, tight heads. 'Carmen' produces softball-sized, red-and-white heads. For the best taste, direct sow in the ground, allowing growing time to extend the harvest after first frost.

CUTTING CELERY (*Apium graveolens*)
This easy-to-grow celery is bred for leaf production, not stems, yet it has the distinctive flavor of celery. Cut 'Par-Cel' at any time. It will quickly replace its parsley-like leaves.

beyond lettuce — more salad greens

Red orach, also known as mountain spinach, is a gorgeous addition to a salad.

DANDELION
(*Taraxacum officinalis*)
Young leaves are great in salad; cook mature ones as you would other greens. Dandelion leaves are a wonderful source of minerals and vitamins. Try 'Dandelion Ameliore', an improved French variety.

MACHE
(*Valerianella locusta*)
Also known as corn salad and lamb's lettuce, it has a slightly nutty, mild flavor that blends well with more tangy greens. Sow early in the spring and throughout the year into fall. You can harvest young leaves or leaves from plants that have gone to seed without their becoming bitter. Substitute mâche in recipes that call for spinach. A milder, nuttier taste will result. Crops mature in about 45 days.

MUSTARD
(*Brassica juncea*)
Mustard leaves are widely variable: curly to flat and maroon red to green. The spicy young leaves are good in salad. Cooking softens the mustardy bite of mature leaves.

NASTURTIUM
(*Tropaeolum majus*)
Nasturtiums are wonderfully decorative and useful. The delightful midgreen leaves add a nice, peppery note to salads.

NEW ZEALAND SPINACH
(*Tetragonia tetragonioides*)
This is not a true spinach. It grows well in less fertile and dry locations. It is also useful for growing in much warmer conditions than spinach. Use in place of spinach in cooked recipes.

RED ORACH
(*Atriplex hortensis*)
Also known as mountain spinach, this is a much more ornamental relative of lamb's quarters. Red orach 'Crimson Plume' makes a decorative red garnish or salad addition. Cooking doesn't remove its color.

PURSLANE
(*Portulaca oleracea* var. *sativa*)
This wonderful weed has recently been rediscovered by cooks and health-food aficionados. It has small, fat, green or golden leaves and an overall Tinker Toy appearance. It is low-calorie, tangy, and crispy and delivers lots of omega-3 fatty acids, and vitamins A and C.

SORREL
(*Rumex acetosa*)
Sorrel is an easily grown perennial famous as the base of French sorrel soup. Include the tart, lemony-flavored, arrow-shaped leaves in an early spring salad.

SPINACH
(*Spinacia oleracea*)
Spinach is a good cool-weather green that's loaded with minerals and vitamins. Spring sow directly in the garden as early as the soil can be worked or in early fall.

'Bloomsdale Longstanding' is a time-tested variety with savoyed, dark green leaves. It's one of the most heat-tolerant.

SWISS CHARD
(*Beta vulgaris*)
Chard is primarily grown for its thick, edible stems. Use young leaves like beet greens, before they develop a prominent midrib. Sauté them quickly or use in a warm salad. Use green chard varieties for cooked stems; red ones can be stringy. 'Monstruoso' is a large-growing, visually striking, Italian variety that has thick, white midribs, recommended for stir-fry or crudités. As ornamentals, the red 'Charlotte' produces great color late in the season. 'Bright Lights', an All-America Selections Winner, offers a heat-tolerant rainbow of hues—orange, pink, red, and purple stems.

Red-veined sorrel is popular as an ornamental, and it's delicious.

Edible flowers seem to be on the cutting edge of the culinary horizon. Eating flowers even seems a bit wild. In fact, eating flowers has a long history.

The Chinese have used daylily flowers for millennia, and Italians have long enjoyed squash blossoms. Edible flowers, particularly the use of rose petals, experienced popularity in Victorian England.

Recently, popular gourmet cooking magazines have begun to feature flowers in salads and other recipes. Some specialty stores and supermarkets offer edible flowers in their produce sections. You can even order them delivered overnight.

The Basics

Consuming flowers can be pleasurable and safe as long as you follow some basic guidelines. The suggestions that follow have been adapted from reigning edible-flower expert Cathy Wilkinson Barash's book, *Edible Flowers: From Garden to Palate*, and her rules of edible flowers.

Don't eat or decorate a plate with any flower you cannot positively identify. Many flowers are edible; many are also poisonous. Consume only organically grown flowers. That means you should never eat flowers from plants at nurseries, florists, or even from roadsides, which may have been sprayed or become contaminated.

People dealing with significant medical challenges and those with allergies, asthma, or hay fever should not consume flowers. Eat only the flower petal, not the stamen and pistil. Start slowly with flowers. Begin by using one kind of flower and consume it only in small quantities.

edible **flowers** for garden and palate

From Picking to Palate

Pick flowers for eating at their peak of perfection. The ideal time of day is in the morning, right after the dew has evaporated. Select flowers that have just opened, avoiding those past their prime and those still in the bud stage.

Store cut flowers as you would those for arrangements. Keep the stems in water in a cool place. Short-stemmed flowers need to be picked and consumed within a few hours. Keep them in the refrigerator. Store them between layers of damp towels placed inside plastic bags. Rinse them off right before using.

They are fragile. Test-wash a few blossoms for discoloration.

The flavor of flowers varies from variety to variety, by season, and the specific location grown. Taste-test flowers from new beds, cultivars, and even the beginning of each season. Like vegetables, the flavor will vary, and you may need to adjust recipes accordingly. There also may be flowers or varieties you don't like. Make your taste test before harvesting quantities of flowers for a recipe. If you don't enjoy the taste, don't eat that flower.

Cut off the bitter white patch at the base of mum, dianthus, English daisy, marigold, and rose petals.

Calendulas are called poor man's saffron—yellow petals impart their color to food.

Hybrid tuberous begonias have a citrusy flavor. They are the only edible begonias.

Extending the Season

The effective storage time for fresh-cut flowers can be measured in hours. Daylilies are the only flowers that have enough substance to withstand freezing. Use the others to make flowery ice cubes, which will enliven any drink.

Once combined into recipes, some flowers will be preserved for longer times. Drying flowers is really the best storage option. Some flavors shift because of the drying process, not unlike with herbs.

Just like drying herbs or flowers for dried flower crafts, dry them in a dark, dry, warm, dust-free place with good air movement. Hang flowers by the stems or dry individual flowers on fine-mesh screening. Once they are dry, store them as you would herbs. Put whole or crumbled flowers in airtight glass containers and store in a cool, dry, and dark location. Use about half, by volume, of the same flower when fresh.

Flower Hit Parade

Herb flowers usually taste like mild-flavored versions of the herb leaves. They are also a great way for gardeners to get their first taste of flowers.

Most kitchen gardens already have plantings of chives (*Allium schoenoprasum*), lavender (*Lavandula* spp.), sage (*Salvia officinalis*), basil (*Ocimum basilicum*), and mint (*Mentha* spp.). Use chive flowers just after they open. The whole flower is strongly flavored, so break it into florets. Cut just the flowers, and chives will continue to rebloom.

Many people prefer the subtler flavor of sage flowers to the leaf. The varieties 'Aurea' and 'Tricolor' rarely flower. Basil is an easily grown annual. The distinctive flavor of mint and clove combined is milder in the flower. Choose mints for appearance and flavor.

Daylilies (*Hemerocallis* spp.) have been consumed for as long as written records have been maintained in China. More people have probably eaten this flower than any other. Golden needles, dried daylily petals, are an ingredient of hot and sour soup.

Harvest daylily flowers the day before they open. Their flavor has been described as being a bit like eggplant or green beans. Daylily buds can be frozen and stored for up to eight months: pick them a day early, blanch for three minutes, plunge into ice water, dry, cool, and pack into freezer bags.

Nasturtium (*Tropaeolum majus*) is a multipurpose plant that's almost foolproof to grow. Its bright and perky flowers liven any planting. The spicy and peppery flavored flowers look and taste great in salads and other recipes. The leaves also are edible, tasting like peppery cress.

Roses have fascinated poets and gardeners for millennia, being cultivated since about 2700 B.C. Carefully select roses that will grow well organically in your area. The best-tasting roses are *Rosa rugosa* and *R. rugosa alba*. A rose must be fragrant to yield flavorful petals. Others worth trying include the old rose species *R. damascena* and *R. gallica*. Taste-test roses, as some have a metallic aftertaste; the sweet flavor varies with touches of cinnamon, mint, or apple.

Colorful pansies are perky in salads or hors d'oeuvres. They have a mild minty flavor.

fruit trees are at home in and have been historically important in the kitchen garden. Quince trees anchor the medieval foursquare garden.

Apples and pears can be trained into decorative and useful backdrops and windscreens. Their spring flowers are as dramatic, decorative, and often as fragrant as other spring-flowering trees. And, a bountiful crop of fruit rewards the grower each fall. Old fruit trees have great character, often becoming living sculptures with gnarled, lichen-covered branches. Shaped trees are a focal point in a garden—espaliered to add geometry to a wall or fence; cordoned into an exclamation point, reaching for the sky.

Fruit Tree Selection Considerations

trees are the most permanent part of the garden; some may last a hundred years or more. Spend the greatest proportion of your planning time deciding which fruit trees, cultivars, and planting locations you will use.

Gardeners can choose from a selection of trees that are disease-resistant, reach smaller ultimate size, yield better fruit quality, and withstand wider temperature extremes. Check with your local Cooperative Extension Service for information on the newest cultivars,

Choose good storage apples that will keep for several months in a cool basement.

grow some tree fruits in your garden

local pests, and varieties best suited to your area.

Apple

apples (*Malus* spp.) have been popular since the early nineteenth century when Johnny Appleseed (John Chapman) championed their merits. This decorative deciduous tree has fragrant spring flowers that give way to crisp, tart, or sweet and juicy late summer or fall fruit.

With over 5,000 varieties to choose from, there is a perfect match for every garden. Heirloom, or antique, cultivars offer the widest array of fruit color and flavor and a bit more of a challenge to the grower. New disease-resistant varieties are easier to grow and make a better pick for the beginning fruit grower. Smaller trees are a better size selection for most gardens. Dwarf varieties grow to about 8×12 feet; semidwarf, 12×20 feet; and standard, 20×30 feet. Plant a second variety of apples to set a full crop of fruit.

Apples need full sun and deep, moist, well-drained soil with a pH of 5.5–7.0. Plant one- or two-year-old trees in early spring with the graft union 2 inches above soil level. Immediately remove any growth that sprouts below the graft. Apples are hardy in zones 3 to 9.

Plant cultivars that are suited to your growing area. If you want to taste a wide variety of apples before deciding which ones to plant, try the Applesource catalog (800-588-3854 or

An espaliered apple tree lends a formal note to an otherwise rustic fence.

www.applesource.com), which lists over 100 varieties of apples for eating. Though taste is always very personal, some favorites in past years include the following (listed in order of ripening): sweet apples: 'Gala', 'Hawaii', 'Jonagold', 'Spigold', 'Mutsu', 'Fuji'; tart apples: 'Akane', 'Prima', 'Jonamac', 'Jonalicious', 'Jonathan', 'Holiday', 'Melrose', 'Idared', 'Granny Smith'; connoisseur favorites: 'Ashmead's Kernel', 'Calville Blanc', 'Cox's Orange Pippin', 'Esopus Spitzenburg', 'Golden Russet', 'Hudson's Golden Gem', 'Newtown Pippin', 'Northern Spy'.

The connoisseur favorites definitely are not modern-looking with nice, smooth waxy skin and shiny, bright colors. They can even be ugly, small, and have rough skin, and have unusual, distinctive flavors.

Cherry

Sweet cherry (*Prunus avium*) and sour cherry or tart cherry (*Prunus cerasus*) trees have lots of gorgeous spring flowers, good foliage, attractive and tasty fruit, and supply winter interest with decorative bark. Sweet cherries grow in zones 5 to 9. The fruit can be eaten raw or cooked.

Sour cherries, or pie cherries, grow in zones 4 to 9 and produce fruit that is usually cooked, though some people enjoy their fresh, tart flavor. Trees grow from 8 to 20 feet tall. 'Montmorency' is a particularly good sour cherry that grows 12 to 15 feet tall.

Plant two varieties for pollination. Plant trees in early spring or in late fall in full sun in well-drained soil with a pH of 6.0 to 8.0. Protect ripening fruit from birds with netting.

Fig

figs (*Ficus carica*) are a plump, delicately sweet fruit—one of the oldest fruits known to man. Trees grow 6 to 20 feet tall and are hardy in zones 7 to 10, to about 10 degrees F. Wrap them "mummy" style, with dry leaves or straw surrounded by burlap, for more protection. Plant figs near a warming wall or espalier on the wall. Self-pollinating, small varieties can be container-grown and moved to a dry location to winter above 15 degrees F. 'Brown Turkey' is the most widely grown variety.

Peach and Nectarine

Peach (*Prunus persica*) and nectarine (*P. persica* var. *nucipersica*) trees produce juicy sweet fruit after showy, pink spring flowers. The main

difference between them is fuzz: peaches have it, nectarines do not. They grow to 20 to 25 feet tall. Prune to hold the maximum height to 10 feet. Plant in full sun in moist, sandy loam with a pH of 6.2 to 6.5. They are generally hardy in zones 5 to 9. Peaches have more cold-tolerant varieties than nectarines.

Pear

Pear (*Pyrus communis*) trees bear fruit of great range: colors of green, yellow, brown, or bright red; skin rough or smooth; flavor mild to rich; and flesh buttery to gritty or crisp to soft. They are attractive trees with snowy white spring flowers, glossy green leaves, and fall fruit. Asian pear is round, crunchy, and crisp; often mistaken for an apple. It is called "apple pear" in most fruit markets.

Pears are hardy in zones 4 to 9; Asian pears in zones 5 to 9. Plant in sun in deep, well-drained soil, pH of 6.0 to 6.5., in two varieties for best pollination and fruit production.

Juicy strawberries are easy to grow and complement any kitchen garden.

Strawberry

Strawberries (*Fragaria* spp.) are the most popular homegrown fruit, probably because they're the easiest to grow.

then a second, lighter crop in autumn. Yield will vary by variety with best flavor produced from plants with the lowest yield. Most plants will give you about 2 cups of fruit per season.

The newest category of

Alpine strawberries grow best with some shade. All prefer a pH of 6.2 to 6.5. Supply adequate moisture throughout the

containers. The variegated leaf form, 'Albo-Marginata', is particularly nice in a strawberry jar.

Purchase bundles of 25 plants of virus-free, dormant plants of everbearing, day-neutral, and June-bearing strawberries for

hold 50 plants. Some nurseries sell a complete system with a sprinkler, frame, bird netting, and plastic cover to extend the season. Remove flowers the first year. Totally renovate beds every three years. Treat day-neutral plants as annuals. With the other types, you can produce new plants from the runners. As the runner grows, cover the end with a little soil and weigh it down with a small rock. Either establish a bed of closely growing plants or move the newly started plants to a new area.

add some berries to the garden

Strawberrries are categorized by when they fruit. June-bearing types produce fruit when days are short: June in the North and earlier in the South.

Everbearing varieties are somewhat smaller plants, a bit fussier, and a little less resistant to soilborne diseases. They produce flavorful, smaller fruit, and, belying their name, do not produce fruit all season long. They give you a spring crop,

strawberries is the day-neutral plants (they produce berries regardless of day length). These tend to have a heavy crop in very early spring, then lighter crops about every six weeks during summer. The final crop comes late summer to fall.

Alpine strawberries (*Fragaria vesca*) yield tiny, very fragrant fruit. The flavor is intense strawberry, with touches of raspberry and pineapple noted by some. They are decorative little plants suited to growing in a wall or as a border.
Growing Strawberries
Plant in full sun in sandy loam enriched with organic matter.

growing season. Day-neutral and everbearing types are hardy in zones 3 to 8; June bearers in zones 3 to 10; and alpines in zones 4 to 10.

Grow alpine strawberries (sometimes called *fraise du bois*) from seed, or beg some crown divisions from a friend. Start the seed early indoors. Remove the oldest plants each year. Fertilize when in active growth. Renovate beds every three years. They are decorative enough to grow in

early spring planting. Carefully plant with the crowns at soil level (follow the diagram that is supplied with your plants). Space plants 18 inches apart and rows 3 feet apart. Or, plant in a strawberry pyramid bed, a 6-foot-diameter circle with two additional inner circles placed at increasing heights. This size will

Everbearing strawberries continue to flower while in fruit.

Raspberry

The rich essence of raspberries (*Rubus idaeus*) is best supplied by growing your own, because this tasty fruit does not ship well. Raspberries are easy to grow in a sunny spot in fertile, well-drained soil. They prefer a slightly acid soil (pH 6.0 to 6.7) and benefit from mulching. Plants need a good supply of moisture to do well. Well-prepared soil with organic amendments (compost, leaf mold, etc.) will produce the best results. Yellow and red raspberries are hardy in zones 3 to 9; purple raspberries in zones 4 to 9; and black raspberries in zones 5 to 9. The black ones are the most heat-tolerant.

Planting Raspberries
Purchase and plant the bareroot, virus-free plants in early spring in rows 4 to 6 foot apart, with plants spaced 15 to 24 inches apart. Shorten the canes to a bud, about 9 inches tall. In the spring, remove mature canes and thin new growth. For ease of harvesting and neatness, support on wires stretched between posts. In a wilder garden, manage in a hill or clump of plants. Mulch with organic materials. Check with extension agents for best local varieties. In the red berry category, 'Heritage' is a widely planted, excellent everbearer; 'Skeena' is a vigorous grower with large fruit; and 'Killarney' is an attractive-looking plant. 'Bristol' is a productive, rich-flavored black raspberry; 'Amber' and 'Fall Gold' are good yellows.

Prune the fruiting canes of raspberries in the fall. Berries will form on new canes.

Blueberry

Blueberries (*Vaccinium corymbosum*) are tasty, succulent, very useful fruit and are easy to grow in proper soil. The hardest requirement to supply is a very acid soil, a pH of 4.0 to 4.8. They will tolerate heavy soils with good drainage but prefer a sandy loam. during during growth and fruiting. They are suitable for container growing where soil is not suitable. When full grown, a plant will yield about 10 quarts of berries per year. Blueberries are hardy in zones 4 to 9. Blueberries are terrific in an informal garden or woodland edge because of the wonderful fall colors. The plants blaze in red, orange, and copper.

Growing Blueberries
Purchase two- or three-year old bareroot plants. Soak them for several hours before planting. Space plants 4 feet apart in rows 10 feet apart. For best fruit production, plant two different varieties. Don't prune the first few years, then only to control rambunctious growth. Fertilize annually and use organic mulch. One of the earliest varieties for harvest is 'Earliblue'. 'Herbert' is one of the best-flavored choices, and 'Bluecrop' delivers a good crop and spectacular fall color.

Wait to pick blueberries until the fruit has been fully colored for a week.

One practical reward for gardening is being able to harvest produce at its peak. The following are a few tips on picking your crops.

ARTICHOKES
The edible part of the artichoke is enclosed inside the immature flower bud. Cut it just before the flower is about to open. The best head is located at the end of the stalk. Many additional heads develop and mature at different times.

ASPARAGUS
By the third year after planting, cut once a week for three weeks. Next year, cut the spears when they are 6 inches high. Harvest by holding each spear in one hand and cutting, about 1 inch below the surface, with a sharp, long, thin-bladed knife.

BEETS
Harvest and use greens before they mature. Harvest the roots throughout the season, from baby to full size.

CABBAGE
Cut only heads that are solid and hard. If you don't want to harvest immediately, give the plant a twist to break the small feeding roots. It can then be left in the garden for some time until needed.

CARROTS
Don't let carrots get old and tough. Pull when young and before tops start to yellow.

CORN
Ears should be full and silk turned brown. Check by peeling back the husk for a quick peek. If the corn hasn't matured enough, close the husk.

EGGPLANT
Cut eggplants when they've colored. Even when they are half their mature size they are edible. As you cut, more fruit will keep growing.

LETTUCE
Harvest lettuce in the morning, when dew is still on the leaves, on the day you will use it. Baby leaves are wonderful in salad. They regrow quickly.

MELONS
Harvest muskmelon and cantaloupe when the melon comes off easily from the stem. It should smell like ripe melon.

PEAS
Pick peas before they fully mature and only minutes before eating them.

PEPPERS
Pick peppers when they have reached the peak of color for the specific variety grown. The flavor of peppers changes dramatically as the color changes.

POTATOES
Start digging potatoes within a month of when the tops wither. That signals that mature tubers have developed. Start digging some distance from the plants and move progressively closer. You will spear fewer potatoes this way.

RADISHES
Pull radishes early, before they get large, hot, and pithy.

TOMATOES
Pick tomatoes when they have attained good color for the specific variety being grown. Store tomatoes at room temperature for the best flavor.

harvest the fruits of your labor

Too Much of a Good Thing

Most kitchen gardeners end up with more than they can possibly use. Share the bounty! Give some of your excess to friends, relatives, and neighbors, or find a soup kitchen or nursing home that could use your bounty. Plant a Row for the Hungry PAR) is a program organized by the Garden Writers Association of

Fresh from the garden, make vegetables into sauces.

Storage

America to encourage gardeners to plant a few extra plants (or an additional row) and donate the extra produce to a food kitchen or shelter. These organizations always have a need for fresh food. To learn where food is needed in your area and what you can do, contact Second Harvest at 312-263-2303 or find Plant-a-Row information at http://www.garden.com or the GWAA Website at http://www.gwaa.org.

Use herbs and edible flowers to make flavored vinegars.

Storing your crop properly will extend your garden harvest into winter. It is the lowest work, highest reward approach to maintaining the flavor and nutritional value of your efforts. Like other facets of gardening, this requires learning a few simple rules—what treatment is best for each vegetable. There are two main groups of vegetables that require two different types of storage: moist and cold or dry and cool. Store only produce free of blemishes and bruises—consume others immediately. Handle each piece carefully, as you would an egg. Don't just toss them into a bushel basket on top of each other. Lay them out separately on

Herbs dry on a screen in preparation for making herbal teas.

crumpled newspaper or sawdust. Don't wash produce before storing. For root crops, leave the roots on and an inch or more of the tops. Leave as much stem of the others as you can.

Cold and Moist Storage

Root crops (beets, carrots, turnips, white potatoes, etc.), fruit (especially apples), and cabbage should have moist and cold storage. Ideal temperatures would be very close to freezing; 35 to 45 degrees F. is best. The easiest way to do this is to leave them in the garden and to dig them when you need them. Flatten the tops of the vegetables and cover them with a bale of

straw or hay. This will prevent the ground from freezing. To harvest in winter, just move the bale of hay and dig your crop. Carrots and leeks will keep this way for the entire winter. Experiment with other crops in your area.

Watch for rodent damage. If you detect damage or activity, harvest the entire crop and store elsewhere.

Try covering cabbage and lettuce with a loose covering (straw, leaves, etc.). Kale, lettuce, and spinach will all tolerate the cold.

A simple storage method is burying a container in the ground

and filling it with layers of vegetables in moist sawdust, sand, or peat moss. A new garbage can with a tight-fitting lid works well. Bury it upright, leaving a few inches out of the ground. Pile about 12 inches of hay or leaves over the top. Cover it all with a tarp or plastic sheet to keep it dry.

Dry and Cool Storage

The few remaining vegetables store best if kept dry and cool. Keep the humidity under 50 percent and temperatures between 50 and 60 degrees F. Onions, pumpkins, and winter squash keep well with this method. Use a spot in the garage or basement with no danger of freezing. Place them so air can circulate around them. Don't stack them in a giant pile on the floor; spread them out on a shelf.

mail-order plant sources

a The Antique Rose Emporium
(P) $5.00
9300 Lueckemeyer Road
Brenam, TX 77833-6453
800-441-0002

b Bear Creek Nursery (P) free
P. O. Box 411
Northport, WA 99157-0411

c Kurt Bluemel, Inc. (P) $3.00
2740 Greene Lane
Baldwin, MD 21013-9523
800-248-7584

d Bountiful Gardens (S) free
18001 Shafer Ranch Road
Willits, CA 95490-9626
707-459-6410

e Burpee, W. Atlee & Co. (S) free
300 Park Avenue
Warminster, PA 18974-0001
800-333-5808

f Busse Gardens (P) $2.00
5873 Oliver Avenue S.W.
Cokato, MN 55321-4229
320-286-2654

g Carroll Gardens (P) $3.00
444 E. Main Street
Westminster, MD 21157
800-638-6334

h The Cook's Garden (S) free
P. O. Box 535
Londonderry, VT 05148
800-457-9703

i Digging Dog (P) $3.00
P. O. Box 471
Albion, CA 95410
707-937-1130

j Evergreen Y. H. Enterprises
(S) $2.00
P. O. Box 17538
Anaheim, CA 92817
714-637-5769

k Henry Field's Seed & Nursery
Company (P) free
415 North Burnett
Shenandoah, IA 51602
605-665-9391

l Forestfarm (P) $4.00
990 Tetherow Rd.
Williams, OR 97544-9599
541-846-7269

m Garden City Seeds (S) free
778 Highway 93 North
Hamilton, MT 59840
406-961-4837

n Goodwin Creek Gardens
(P, S) $2.00
P. O. Box 83
Williams, OR 97544
503-846-7357

o The Gourmet Gardener (S) free
8650 College Boulevard
Overland Park, KS 66210
913-345-0490

p Gurney Seed & Nursery
Company (S) free
110 Capital Street
Yankton, SD 57079
605-665-4451

q Harris Seeds (S) free
P. O. Box 22960
Rochester, NY 14692-2960
800-514-4441

r Heirloom Seeds (S) $1.00
P. O. Box 245
West Elisabeth, PA 15088-0245
412-384-0852

s High Country Gardens (P) free
2902 Rufina Street
Santa Fe, NM 87505-2929
800-925-9387

t Heronswood Nursery Ltd.
(P) $4.00
7530 NE 288th Street
Kingston, WA 98346
360-297-4172

u Hudson, J. L., Seedsman
(S) $1.00
Star Route 2, Box 337
La Honda CA 94020

v Jackson & Perkins Co. (P) free
P. O. Box 1028
Medford, OR 97501
800-292-4769

w Johnny's Selected Seeds
(S) free
Foss Hill Road
Albion, ME 04910-9731
207-437-4301

x D. Landreth Seed Co. (S) free
P. O. Box 6426
Baltimore, MD 21230
800-654-2407

hh Owen Farms (P) $2.00
2951 Curve-Nankipoo Road
Ripley, TN 38063-6653
901-635-1588

ii Park Seed Company (S) free
One Parkton Avenue
Greenwood, SC 29647-0001
800-845-3369

jj The Pepper Gal (S) $2.00
P. O. Box 23006
Ft. Lauderdale, FL 33307-3006
945-537-5540

kk Pinetree Garden Seeds
(S) free
Box 300
New Gloucester, ME 04260
207-926-3400

ll Prairie Nursery (P) free
P. O. Box 306
Westfield, WI 53964
608-296-3679

mm Raintree Nursery, Inc.
(P) free
391 Butts Road
Morton, WA 98356
360-496-6400

nn Redwood City Seed Company
(S) $1.00
P. O. Box 361
Redwood City, CA 94064
415-325-7333

oo Richters Herbs (S, P) free
357 Highway 47
Goodwood, Ontario
Canada L0C 1A0
905-640-6677

pp Ronniger's Seed & Potato Co.
(P, S) free
P. O. Box 307
Ellensburg, WA 98926

qq Seed Savers Exchange
(S) free
3076 North Winn Road
Decorah, IA 52101
319-382-5990

rr Seeds Blum (S) $3.00
HC 33 Box 2057
Boise, ID 83706
800-742-1423

metric conversions

U.S. Units to Metric Equivalen

To Convert From	Multiply By	To Get
Inches	25.4	Millimetres
Inches	2.54	Centimetres
Feet	30.48	Centimetres
Feet	0.3048	Metres
Yards	0.9144	Metres
Square inches	6.4516	Square centimetres
Square feet	0.0929	Square metres
Square yards	0.8361	Square metres
Acres	0.4047	Hectares
Cubic inches	16.387	Cubic centimetres
Cubic feet	0.0283	Cubic metres
Cubic feet	28.316	Litres
Cubic yards	0.7646	Cubic metres
Cubic yards	764.55	Litres

To convert from degrees Fahrenheit (F) to degrees Celsius (C), first subtract 32, then multiply by ⁵⁄₉.

Metric Units to U.S. Equivalents

To Convert From	Multiply By	To Get
Millimetres	0.0394	Inches
Centimetres	0.3937	Inches
Centimetres	0.0328	Feet
Metres	3.2808	Feet
Metres	1.0936	Yards
Square centimetres	0.1550	Square inches
Square metres	10.764	Square feet
Square metres	1.1960	Square yards
Hectares	2.4711	Acres
Cubic centimetres	0.0610	Cubic inches
Cubic metres	35.315	Cubic feet
Litres	0.0353	Cubic feet
Cubic metres	1.308	Cubic yards
Litres	0.0013	Cubic yards

To convert from degrees Celsius to degrees Fahrenheit, multiply by ⁹⁄₅, then add 32.

SS Seeds of Change (S) free
P. O. Box 15700
Santa Fe, NM 87506-5700
888-762-7333

tt Select Seed (S) $3.00
180 Stickney Hill Rd.
Union, CT 06076-4617
860-684-9310

uu Shepherd's Garden Seeds
(S) free
30 Irene Street
Torrington, CT 06790
860-496-9624

VV R. H. Shumway's (S) free
P. O. Box 1
Graniteville, SC 29829
803-663-9771

WW Siskiyou Rare Plant Nursery
(P) $3.00
2825 Cummings Rd.
Medford, OR 97501-1538
541-746-3922

XX Southern Exposure Seed
Exchange (S) $2.00
P. O. Box 170
Earlysville, VA 22936
804-973-4703

yy Stark Brothers Nurseries and
Orchards Co. (P) free
P. O. Box 10
Louisiana, MO 63353-0010
800-325-4180

ZZ Stokes Seeds, Inc. (S) free
P. O. Box 548
Buffalo, NY 14240
716-695-6980

aaa Territorial Seed Company
(S) free
P. O. Box 157
Cottage Grove, OR 97424-0061
541-942-9547

bbb Thompson & Morgan, Inc.
(S) free
P. O. Box 1308
Jackson, NJ 08527-0308
800-274-7333

ccc Tomato Growers Supply
Company (S) free
P. O. Box 2237
Fort Myers, FL 33902
941-768-1119

ddd Vermont Bean Seed Co.
(S) free
Garden Lane
Fair Haven, VT 05743
803-663-0217

eee André Viette Farm &
Nursery (P) free
P. O. Box 1109
Fishersville, VA 22939
800-575-5538

fff Well-Sweep Herb Farm
(P, S) $2.00
205 Mt. Bethel Road
Port Murray, NJ 07865
908-852-5390

ggg Wayside Gardens (P) free
1 Garden Lane
Hodges, SC 29695-0001
800-845-1124

hhh Chris Weeks Peppers
(S) $1.00
P. O. Box 3207
Kill Devil Hills, NC 27948

iii Weiss Brothers Nursery
(P) free
11690 Colfax Highway
Grass Valley, CA 95945
916-272-7657

jjj White Flower Farm (P) free
PO Box 50
Litchfield, CT 06759-0050
800-503-9624

(P) Plants	(B) Bulbs
(S) Seed	($0) Price of catalog

plant index

Page references in *italics* indicate photographs.

Acknowledgements

We wish to thank the following people
whose gardens originally appeared in
the pages of *Country Home*® *Country
Gardens*:

Bruce Burstert and Robert Raymond
  Smith
John and Marie Butler
Robert Dash
Jacque Eggan
Mary Fisher
Clarabel Kent
Sarah Pearl and Barry Sachs
Charleen Perry
Dean Riddle
Cris Spindler
Evalyn and Tony Walsh
Dick and Diane Weaver
Genie White

And thanks to Stephen Kelly for the use
of his garden for cover photography.